HUNTING LORE

by
JARIT MELUDA

translated by
ANTHONY RICHARDS

BORNEO LITERATURE BUREAU

CONTENTS

FISHING

Chapter		Page
I	Hook and Line	1
II	Nets	16
III	Traps	24
IV	Basket-fishing and Fish-ponds	39
V	Fish Poisons and the way they are used ...	41
VI	Fish Poison: The Law of the Rajah ...	50
VII	The Management of a Fish-drive ...	52

HUNTING ON LAND

VIII	Do's and Dont's with a Gun	61
IX	Hunting	66
X	Nets and Trapping ...	76
XI	Other Methods of Hunting ...	89
XII	Ways of Cooking	95

Appendix

A	... ...	96
B	... ...	97
C	... ...	105
D	... ...	108
E	... ...	112

TRANSLATOR'S NOTE

"My husband has gone up the hill with a shotgun this evening so perhaps there will be a hare for supper." So writes a friend from England, and says she is looking forward to the fishing season when she too can join in the hunt. I suppose there are people everywhere who say, "Its my delight on a shiny night, in the season of the year.....", but in Sarawak the dangers are not from gamekeepers.

Here, where so many people have to rely on their own skill and knowledge to get a bare living from river and forest, the hunt is a very serious matter. There may be dangers from crocodile, snake or black bear, and there is always a risk of mosquito-borne diseases, wounds from thorns and falls, or eye and ear trouble from prolonged diving. The work is hard because material for the necessary equipment has to be collected from the forest and it all has to be made up by hand.

Ibans go on hunting expeditions sometimes for the purpose of allaying anxiety or sorrow, to recover a mental balance they feel they may lose and to put themselves at rest again, as they say, 'nyamai diri'. To go into the wilderness and return safely with the catch adds to one's self-respect. Victory over a bear does more than this:

it gives a reputation for great courage and skill.

This little book I have translated was written in Iban by Jarit Meluda. He is widely known as an expert fisherman. He is also a skilful trapper and a hardworking farmer. His main interest is in fending for his family by his own efforts, often solitary. Although there is a great deal about tuba-fishing in this book, he does not in practice favour it or any other undertaking, like netting deer, which requires a large party, and a lot of organisation, and may lead to an improvident slaughter.

Patient watching leads to an understanding of your quarry so that you can kill more surely, and according to your needs. You use your craft to fill the pot; not for its own sake or for sport. This applies even more strongly among the more old-fashioned people far up-river, whose beliefs require them to use all kinds of ritual actions and words to ensure success, as well as to avoid enraging the gods of forest and flood under whose protection and leadership the wild things live. The only mention of these matters is in the description of a tuba-fishing.

Translation also showed the need for more explanation and detail. It is a rare craftsman who can write down everything and dispense with demonstration. I have shown how the traps work in illustrations and have added to the original in several places.

    I am grateful to Mr. B.E. Smythies and Mr. P.S. Ashton of the Forest Department for identifying trees and plants, and to Mr. Ong Kee Bian of the Agriculture Department for the list of fishes. I was unable to identify all the insects and have therefore omitted their scientific names: it seems that almost any insect of reasonable size and meatiness will do for bait provided its case or shell is not too hard. This means that the majority used are various kinds of grasshopper. I know of no reason why the red weaver-ant,'kesak', is so popular in the world of fish.

    I hope that others will assist in filling some of the obvious gaps in this contribution. There is nothing here about edible plants and seasonings. Blowpipes are barely mentioned because they have been replaced by the twelve-bore shotgun. The art and ritual needed for making the poison for the darts would need a separate study.

    However, this book is about the more humdrum, homely, "down-river" practice of an art. For those who have no opportunity or, perhaps, desire to acquire any of these skills or try them, this translation may arouse their interest and tell something of the knowledge and careful labour that is needed before food can be won from the forest.

Anthony Richards.

INTRODUCTION

This handbook sets out to explain very briefly various ways of seeking food from the river and the forest. We have only described methods we know at first hand, and which are in common use in Sarawak.

We started to write about fishing. Afterwards, because people must also hunt upon the land and in the forest, we added a second part to tell you about shooting and trapping wild animals to eat.

All the methods described are from the Rejang. These methods vary from place to place and in other rivers quite different methods are to be found. But we have not attempted to include all of them: either because they are uncommon, because we have never seen them for ourselves, or because they are not used nowadays by anyone who is likely to read this book. A few such other ways of doing things to get fish or game are, however, mentioned in Chapter II under the heading of, 'Other methods of Hunting'.

The reason for writing this book at all was to help preserve the old skill in such matters and prevent it dying out. We hope that those who read it will add to it anything they know and so keep the knowledge alive.

We hope, too, that some who read will find they can learn some new dodges from it, which will be useful to them. But if not, let the children read it so that they will know and understand some of the things the older people spend a good deal of time on. Then, when the younger ones understand, they will not be a hindrance and the older folk will no longer be unwilling to take them out to help. Also, if the young people know how to hunt, they need never feel helpless in the forest or fear they will go hungry.

Finally, we say how grateful we are to all those who helped us in various ways. There are too many to mention each one by name, but we thank them all here.

JARIT MELUDA.
ANTHONY RICHARDS.

At Simanggang,
12th January, 1961.

FISHING

A description of various ways of fishing in the Rejang.

CHAPTER I

HOOK AND LINE

Fish hooks are numbered according to size from one to twenty, number twenty being the smallest. The price ranges from ten cents for four hooks of the smallest size, to ten cents for two hooks of the number eleven size, which is the biggest likely to be of use in a river.

These prices are not certain, of course, because you may have to pay more the further you are from a big bazaar, and where the one or two shops can charge what they like.

BAIT.

Any of these can be used as bait:

Insects	Rice
Red Ants	Fermented rice
Red Ants' eggs	Cooked rice
Grasshoppers and locusts	Padi husk

Others

Worms	Frogs
Pig's guts	Young birds

Others

Fowl's guts   Snails
Duck's guts   Fish

Many fruits and berries can also be used, so long as they are small and grow near the water you are fishing (Appendix A).

STAKE-LINES (ginti ujak)

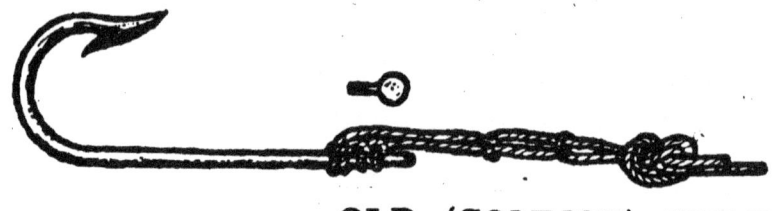

OLD (COMMON) KNOT

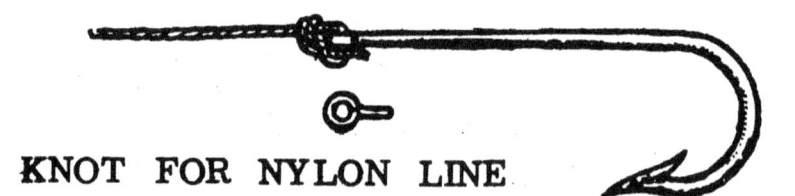

KNOT FOR NYLON LINE

First buy your hooks and thread, and tie a yard or so of line to each hook. Then get small bamboos, five or six feet long and about the thickness of a finger. Tie one of the lines to each bamboo a couple of feet from the butt end.

The best time to put out your stake-lines is after rain, when the river is rising and muddy. Use worms for bait.

The place to set the bamboo stakes is in shallow water, where the river bank is covered with bushes, or there is a heap of driftwood and leaves. It is no good setting them anywhere and anyhow. If the place is dark and shady the fish will be bolder to take your bait, but they become suspicious if they can see everything too clearly. The fish know very well how to look after themselves and the ones we catch are only the ones whose luck has run out.

There are so many things that can be used as bait that they cannot all be mentioned, but the best bait for stake-lines is worms.

TREE-LINES

Having got your thread and your hooks, tie the hooks on lines about four feet long.

Tie the lines to the ends of thin branches that bend easily and spring back, so that the thread won't break if a fish takes the bait. Choose a place where the water is running pretty fast: this will blur the line so the fish don't see it till too late. If the water is still, or you set the lines in a backwater, the fish have time to think and they will see the line and sheer off.

All sorts of things can be used as bait for these lines, such as rubber nuts, wild fig fruit or anything else in season that the fish are eating. The baited hooks must lie two or three inches under water. When using this method, hide the bait with a drifted leaf so that everything looks as if it came there naturally and the fish don't suspect danger.

It is also a good idea to darken the thread with cutch or a black dye so that it can't be seen by the fish.

ROD AND LINE (fixed)

Besides hook and line, for this you need a good strong tapering palm rib of a particular kind known as 'ridan', for a rod.

The best kind, if you can find it, is one that grows with a nest of stinging ants 'komusu', or wasps 'pantak', on it. I don't know why this makes the rods so good, but our ancestors found it out long ago, and it is so.

'Ridan' is best, but if there is none to be had you can use bamboo or rotan or any kind of wood that has a whippy end. Get 'ridan' if you can, though.

Tie a float to the line so that, if a fish nibbles or takes the bait you get warning and can be ready. You can make one out of the rib of a wild sago leaf or 'ridan', or anything else that floats well. But the hook itself must have a sinker of lead, or a stone, or an old nail, or anything small and heavy.

The float should be about the size of your thumb and made so that it can be eased up or down the line according to the depth of water, for the hook should hang near the bottom. It tells you when you have hooked a fish so that you are ready and can strike with the rod.

The best time for fishing this way is in the evening, but it's not much good after rain or a strong wind because then a lot of insects will have fallen on the water and the fish will have plenty else to eat. But, if it is a calm evening and there has been no storm, the fish will be hungry and look for food.

Set rods and lines in a place shaded by bushes, where the water is not too strong nor yet running too slow; but you must judge this for yourself by experience.

For rod and line fishing, it's as well to mix the bait with earth: it helps to trick the fish into taking it.

A lot of people bait their hooks the wrong way. It must be done carefully and not just anyhow. The bait must cover the hook completely so that the fish can't see it, but they can only see the bait. The baited hook must be made to look more natural still by having a drifted leaf or twig added to it or put near it, so that the fish suspect no harm.

Again, you can use many kinds of bait: worms, prawn paste 'blachan', or meat. But if you use meat, or prawn paste, or fish, it's better to roast it a little first so that the fish are attracted by the smell of it.

DRIFT-LINES

To use this method you start by getting 'pulai' wood, or any other very light wood that floats easily. Shape the pieces of wood to look like ducks or other birds, according to your skill, so that they look well.

The time to use drift-lines is in the early morning or late evening. The bait can be anything you know the fish are fond of in the stretch of water you are fishing: banana, fig, or anything commonly eaten by the fish will do. Best of all is illipe nut 'engkabang', pounded small and mixed with cooked rice, for it smells very sweet and is soon found by the fish.

The lines should hang from the floats about eighteen inches deep. Don't make them too long, for fear they will catch on a sunken log. Let the floats with their hooks and lines drift down the middle of the river. When they have gone far enough, follow them gently in a boat so that you are there to collect the fish when one of the ducks begins to bob. It is best if the lines drift down where the water ripples in a narrow place and moves swiftly, so that the fish will nibble at something they think is naturally drifting in the river.

SNARE-HOOKS

A snare-hook is fixed up just like a bird-snare, only it is set in the water and armed with a hook instead of a noose. First of all, choose a rod of small bamboo, or a stick of wood of any kind so long as it is strong and springy. Take a line about five feet long; tie it to the thin end of the springy rod and stick the butt-end into the river bank.

Now get a stout stick, make a notch in it and drive it in firmly under the water. Take another piece of stick, make a notch in that too and fix it to the line. Bend the springy rod over and hook the two notched sticks together.

If a fish takes the bait he separates the notched sticks and releases the trap: the rod springs straight and lifts him out of the water just as if you were there to do it yourself.

When you set one of these snares, the bait should show a little, but the line should be hidden by covering it with earth or a bit of wood. And the bait should be half hidden by a leaf, so that the fish will be bold enough to snatch at it.

A fish, you see, has no hands: but he has a tail he uses instead. If you watch him closely, you will see that he flicks at the bait with his tail to see what happens, before he takes it and eats it. Sometimes, of course, he tries it with his tail and then swims off without touching it again. That's why we have to be careful and patient when fishing and why we must learn when the fish are hungry: for it's no good going to the river and catching nothing.

These snares are best used morning or evening, but not too late or the fish will have gone into the deeper pools. Fish always stay quiet and sleep from about mid-morning till early afternoon, when they come up again looking for food.

If the river is in flood they go on feeding without bothering to rest. So that if you go fishing when the water is high you should be in luck; if you use slack water near the bank, that is. But your bait will be different according to whether the water is rising or going down.

LONG LINE

If you live a long way up-river, far from any shops and want to use this method, you must first get some 'entenang' bark. Divide it into strips thin enough and roll it into a cord as tight as you can. But if there is 'tengang' it is better.

Nowadays, though, there are all sorts of ready-made cordage to be had; people won't be bothered to make it for themselves, but come to rely on the shops where they can buy it more easily.

The time to use a long line is when the water is low. The line may be fouled by driftwood when the water is high, for it has several hooks on it. Also, the line must be weighted with a stone so that it sinks, otherwise it won't work properly.

Cast the line at the head of a pool. The fish come swimming to and fro that way to look for food and will come upon the bait. Then, if their luck is out, you've got them.

If you cast at the lower end of a pool you will get fish too, but not so many because the water is more still there, and the fish have time to think.

Any number of people know different ways of catching fish, but some take no trouble to study the ways of fish. You don't get many fish if you cast at the lower end of a pool because the only fish who will be attracted by your bait will be the few who come up from the next pool below: even they may pass it by as they go into the pool above the bait.

Use different bait for different states of the water. If it is rising, use worms. Otherwise the best to use is a fruit or berry that grows nearby and is eaten by the fish, such as 'kara', or 'engkabang'.

If you use 'engkabang', it is a good thing to bury the nuts in the ground for two or three nights beforehand, so that the fish will not know they are fresh but will think they are old wind-fails washed away by the river as it rises. Also, of course, the bait should be used some distance below the tree where it **grows**.

Always take care that the hook itself does not show at all. If it does, you may still get fish, but not many and then only the ones who are rash and careless.

Then, too, the length of line and the size of the hooks must match the size of the river. But each one must judge for himself in this.

ROD AND LINE (casting)

The rod and line in this case is the same as that used for fixed rod and line but it is not fixed in position, and you use the rod to cast the hook up and down-stream in pools and bays and any other likely place where there may be fruit drifting that the fish eat. However, unlike the fixed rod, this one has no sinker-weight for the hook, nor any float.

A calm clear evening is a good time. So is the early morning when birds and small animals are out after fruit and berries, because some gets dropped and falls into the water to be snapped up by the fish. Then is the time to paddle slowly and quietly up under the tree where the fruit is growing and cast there. The fish will think your bait is just another fruit falling, and will take it.

If you do not get to know dodges like this, you waste a lot of time for nothing and come home hungry and empty-handed.

If there has been a storm your catch with rod and line will be poor, because the fish will have had plenty to eat already, swallowing everything that was knocked down by the rain and wind. You will have a much better chance if the day is fine. It will be better still in the dusk because that is when the fish mostly feed, but you must then cast in the main current, at the top of a pool.

Do not use too heavy a line or it can be seen by the fish. For up-river fishing the best line to use is made of 'kikat', but nowadays people don't bother with it and simply buy ready-made stuff from the bazaar.

Handling the rod is easiest if you sit in the bows of the boat: you can cast left and right and in front of you then.

Red Ants' eggs, locust grasshopper grubs, or anything the fish take is good for bait.

This method gives the best results a long way up-river. It is not very good in deep water down-river.

ROD AND REEL

This is a popular way of fishing from an outboard or launch, but is very seldom used by up-river people. Bread, in some form, is used as bait and the hooks are larger, about number eight; but choose them according to the size of fish you see or know are to be caught in the place.

People who live in towns fish this way, either from the bank, or a handy rock, or from a motor boat, just as a sport and to pass the time. The rods and reels can be bought in the towns.

Besides bread, all sorts of other bait can be used and you can try a few casts at any time, without troubling about the weather.

The reel is fixed to the butt-end of the rod and has a long length of line wound on it. If a fish takes the hook, it struggles and the fine line runs out off the reel. You can check and reel it in again, and so play the fish until it is tired out. Nevertheless, you must learn to do this properly or the line will always part and you will lose fish and hook and all.

This way is good for fishing at sea, but is not much good up-river.

HAND LINE

This has only one hook and a lead weight. If you have no lead, a stone will do, for this is really only a quick makeshift when you find fish but have no proper tackle with you, nor time to get it.

You can hold the line, or tie it to a branch, or to a stick stuck in the river-bed. One way is as good as another.

You must weight the hook so that when you throw it, it will sink as soon as it hits the water. Also the line must not be too short or the hook will finish up too close to the splash of the weight, in which case the fish will be startled.

SPINNERS (and spoon-bait)

First you must make your spinner by beating out a bit of shiny silver or tin, so that it has a twist in it to make it turn about and spin as you draw it through the water on your line.

This will make the fish chase after it and snap at it: but the hook is on the end of it.

A spinner is not like an ordinary hook, for there is no other bait.

'Ridan' is best for the rod, but if you are hard put to it you can make do with bamboo or rotan or other springy wood.

A spinner is effective in the upper reaches of a river, where you can use a boat. You cast the spinner from the bows and draw it through swift currents and slack water, across pools and between rocks wherever fish may lie.

CHAPTER II

NETS

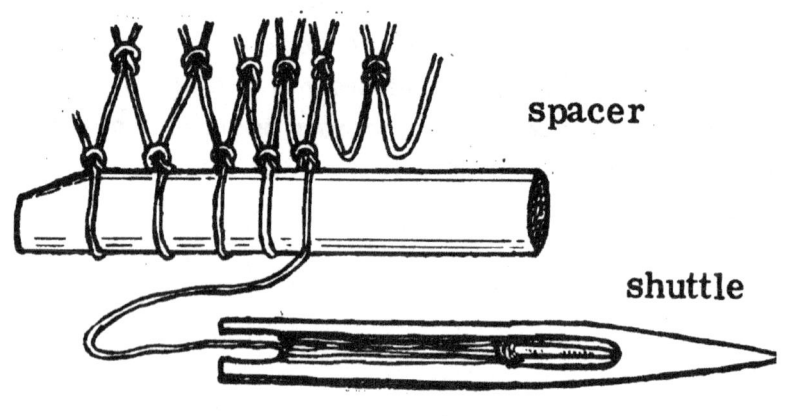

spacer

shuttle

NET MAKING

COARSE CAST-NETS

This net is quickly made because it is coarse, but it must not be too roughly made or the knots will be spaced unevenly and the net unreliable. The net should be fifteen to twenty-five feet deep, according to the average depth of the river where you want to use it.

Cast the net when the river is rising high because then the big fish come searching for food along the banks. But don't try it without choosing good weather, as well as good water.

FINE CAST-NETS

A small mesh net needs fine thread and therefore takes more careful work and a long time to make. You cannot hurry the work or it will be wasted and you won't have much idea of when it will be finished.

Cast the net in the evening, for the last couple of hours of daylight. As darkness falls the fish can see you less and less (and your shadow is less likely to frighten them). Put down bait mixed with earth before casting: this gets the fish attracted to one spot. Padi-husk and fermented rice are often good, but usually whatever you find works the trick. Mark the place carefully where you put the bait, so that you know where to make your cast.

In small streams it is as well to clear bushes and driftwood from the chosen stretch of water to avoid getting the net caught up. Then put down the bait, which in that case can be ants, red ants or termites, but always mixed with earth so that the fish will be slow to finish it.

When the fish have gathered to nose about at the earth, and are eating the bait, move up steadily but very gently to cast your net.

STAKE-NETS

A stake-net is made very like a cast-net, but only half as big, as if a cast-net had been cut in two. The mouth of it should not be more than eighteen feet wide or you won't be able to raise it easily.

As its name implies, a stake-net is not cast from the hand, but is fixed in the stream between a pair of bamboos or round poles. The mouth is set up-stream because the net is used to trap fish that are coming down. It is used particularly when tuba-fishing is in progress, to catch the fish that would otherwise escape down-stream from the poison.

Tie a thread to the butt-end of the net as a tell-tale: then you will know as soon as a fish runs into it.

Stake the net in the main current because that is the quickest way for a frightened fish to escape down-stream.

In the evening is a good time for fishing this way, but a bright moon will give you a poor catch.

The Agriculture Department have published a booklet on the maintenance of cast-nets.

SEINE-NETS (fine and coarse)

There are two sorts. The fine one is made to catch 'enseluai' and other small fish: the coarse one is for the bigger fish. Both are made the same way, but the finer the net, the longer it takes to make.

The coarse-net is usually set across the mouth of a side stream if it is not running too fast. However, if the water is running strongly, find a bay of slack water, or a deep place where the stream is less swift. Wherever you put it, make sure there are no logs or brushwood to foul the net.

The fine net should be set at the water's edge, to catch small fish as they search for food in shallow water. Often they will be escaping from bigger fish who eat them, and will then rush into the fine net and be caught. For this reason it is a good dodge to use both nets together; the coarse-net in the stream and the fine one by the bank. Then the big fish who eat their smaller fellows will get caught by the coarse-net, and the little ones by the other.

The fine net will serve as bait once a few small fish are caught in it, and the bigger fish will dash after them, only to run into the coarse-net.

There is another sort which is very coarse indeed. It is made three or four fathoms long and about the same depth, with weights of lead or stone on the bottom edge. Don't make the weights too big or the net will be unmanageable. This net is laid in slack water or in a steep-sided pool so that its lower edge is on the bottom, and the upper edge is held up by a bamboo.

Tie it by a single cord to the end of a branch or a sapling, so that you can lift it from time to time to see if anything has been caught. When the fish are feeding, they will search about along the bottom and run into the net.

This is really a ground-net, and is useful in the headwaters. I've never seen it used by Ibans but the Kayans in the Ulu Rejang use it a lot.

Nylon fishing-line is now used for making these nets and they have become popular so quickly that there is a grave risk of rivers being over-fished. The ones I have seen most were fairly coarse-meshed, it is true, but fine nets are being made of twisted nylon thread as well.

The fishing-line nets take longer to make because extra turns have to be put into each knot to prevent it slipping. Having passed the free-end up through the loop it must be taken two or three times round both parts of the loop before bringing it down through to complete the knot. Once made, these nets do not need treatment with 'samak' to prevent rot, nor do they need drying after use. So long as they are not set too tight or too slack, which can result in tearing or bursting, the nets will be long lasting.

A further method of fishing has now been adopted which is by the use of a harpoon gun. The Ibans have always made beautiful gun-stocks, and now they use these as the basis of home made spring-guns for fish. The spring is a strip of rubber, heavy motor tyre for preference, and the harpoon attached by a length of fishing line. If you can afford to buy a mask and frogmen's flippers, so much the better, but no fish is now safe even in the deepest pool and there is no need to use tuba-root. Before long there will no doubt be reports of shooting "accidents" occuring under water as they do now upon land.

POCKET-NETS (hand-nets)

· These don't take long to make because they are small and need only a small amount of work and material. The kind called 'tabir' is tapered off rather like a cast-net, but the 'tanggok' kind is shallower and more rounded.

They are given a rotan rim and handle shaped like a badminton racquet.

These nets are used when a river is poisoned for fish, and for working small streams. Women and children don't go in for spearing fish much, so they have these nets made for them to use at tuba-fishing. But they don't catch fish of any size with them.

DIP-NETS

These are like stake-nets in shape but are handled from the bows of a boat. You drift down past landing places, under trees or sometimes in the main current, looking for fish moving upstream. The pocket of the net has a small cord as a tell-tale, so that when a fish runs into it you know it at once and can take the fish out.

The net can be used in any part of a river except where it is too small; too shallow for the net or too narrow for a boat.

The net is held between two sticks in a V-shape. The sticks cross at the butt, where you hold them, but their other ends are tapered for lightness and curve inwards so that the further edge of the net is held taut.

GIANT CAST-NET

This net is very seldom used where fish are at all scarce, and it is pointless to use it at all where the fish are only small. But in swift water, far up-stream, and where there are plenty of fish, people use this method.

Any fish that is caught in this way will be big enough to flip over-board again unless you chop him on a block and kill him.

Any fish weighing less than three pounds will slip through, because the net is made so coarse. Nevertheless, in the far headwaters, the net is good; it sinks very quickly and does not have to be watched for a long time, so that it can be cast often.

CHAPTER III

TRAPS

FENCE-TRAP (kilong)

First get bamboo, some rotan to bind it into shape, and a length of creeper for the rim.

When you have got the makings of the trap together, split the bamboo into thin strips and shave off the sharp edges with your knife. Then split the rotan and peel off the sharp edges of that, ready for binding the bamboo strips together. If you have bracken 'resam', anywhere near, use that and do not go to the trouble of rotan, because the bracken is much quicker to use and lasts longer in water or on the ground.

When everything is ready, you can start forming the trap. Be careful, though, not to lay the strips opposite ways, butt to tip, head to tail, because if you do there will be a curse on the thing, so that it will never catch any fish. At least, so our people have always said: it's wicked to do such a thing. But whatever way you look at it, if the strips do not lie all the same way, it is clumsy work: the result will be a botched job and not something neat that you can be proud of.

FENCE TRAP

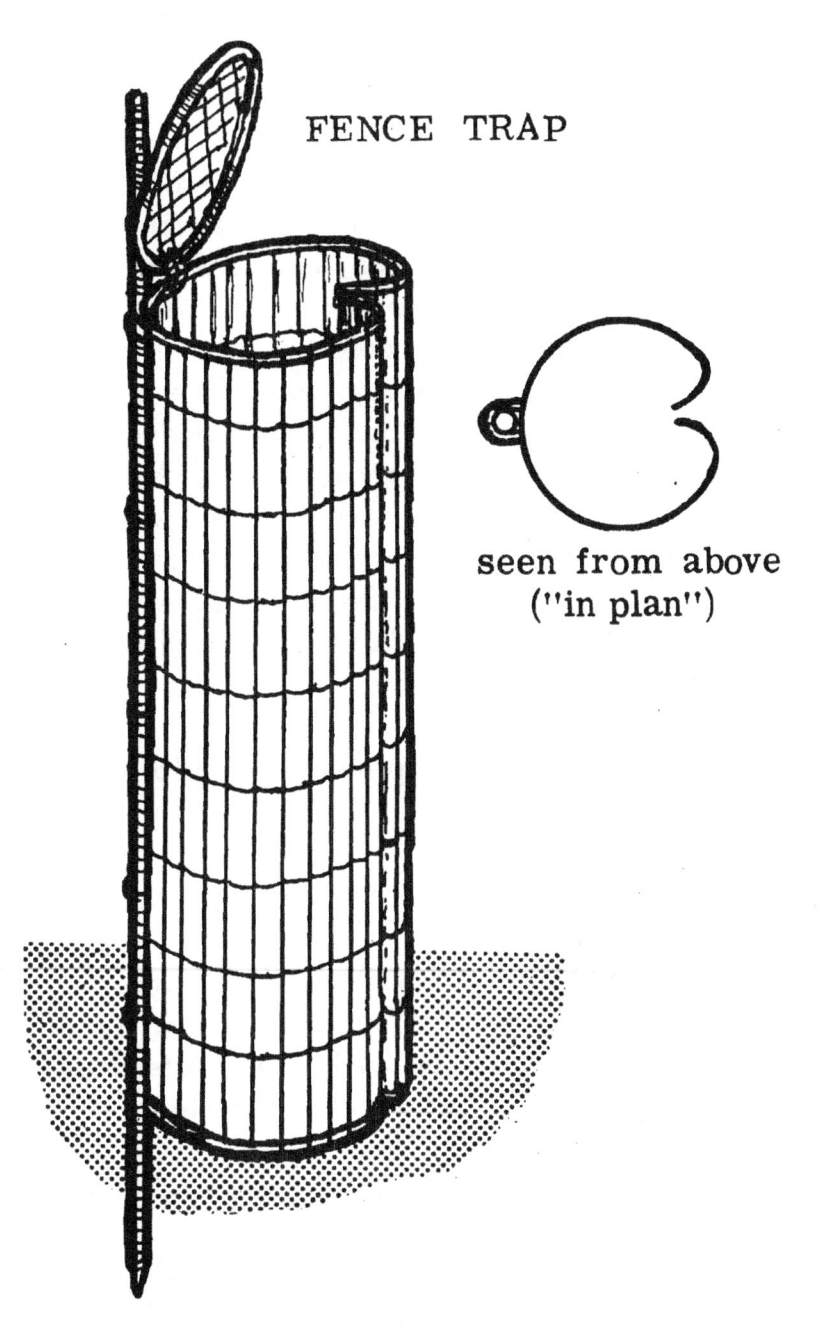

seen from above
("in plan")

To get the best results, set this trap when the water is high in flood.

Pick a place where the water is running fairly fast, but not so fast that the trap won't stay where you put it: for instance, beside where the ground juts out a little into the stream. But you must choose carefully, because the trap will not work if it is put down just anywhere. The place should be a hollow of the bank that is over-grown, for too open a place is no good: it should be just out of a run of fast water, because if the water is slack the fish can turn round and get out of the trap again. This is very different from the setting of an ordinary round trap, but then its a different shape too, being tall, with a long mouth.

Carefully set, this trap will catch a lot more fish than the ordinary sort.

LOG-TRAP

This is made with the same materials and in exactly the same way as a fence-trap but it is a different shape. It can be set in quiet water too because a fish cannot get out of it once he is in, as he can from a fence-trap.

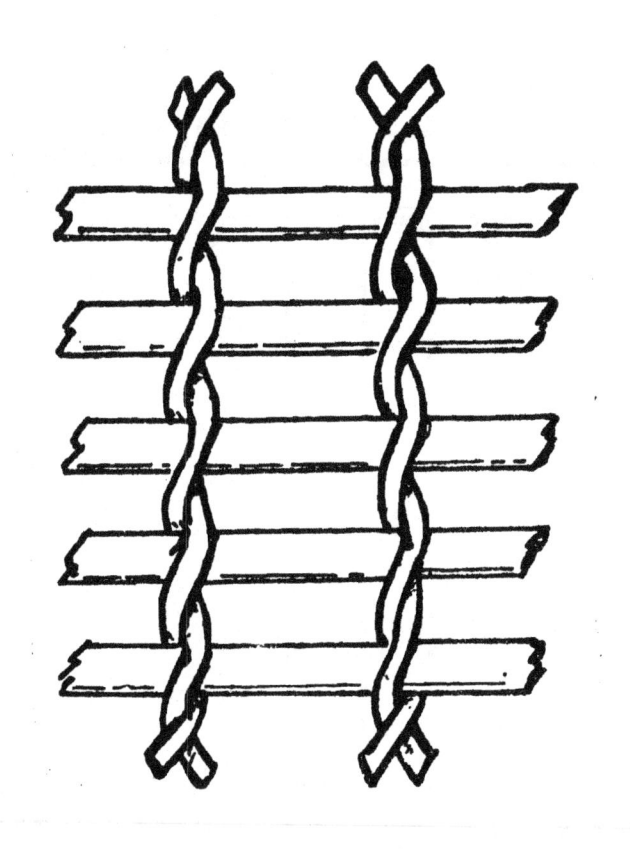

FISH TRAP WEAVE
(use right hand turns)

near side

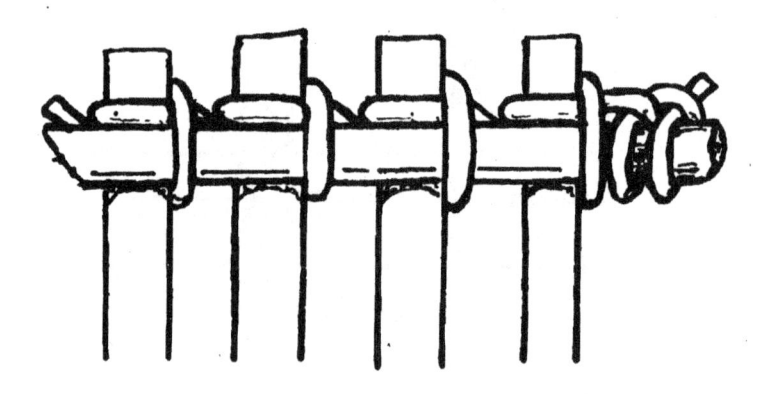

WEAVING THE RIM AND INNER CONE

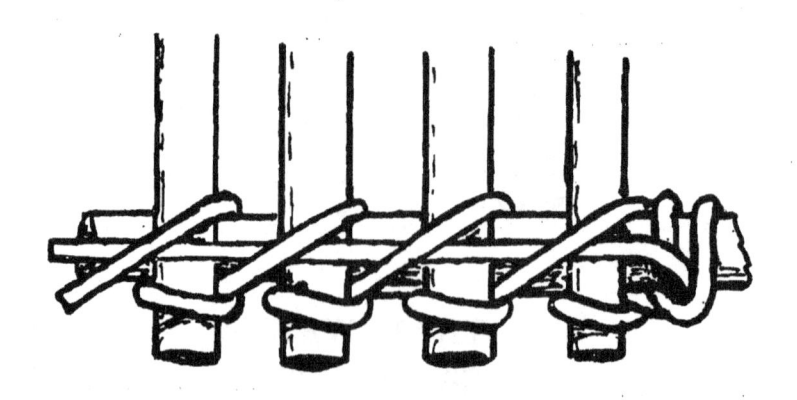

far side

LOG TRAP

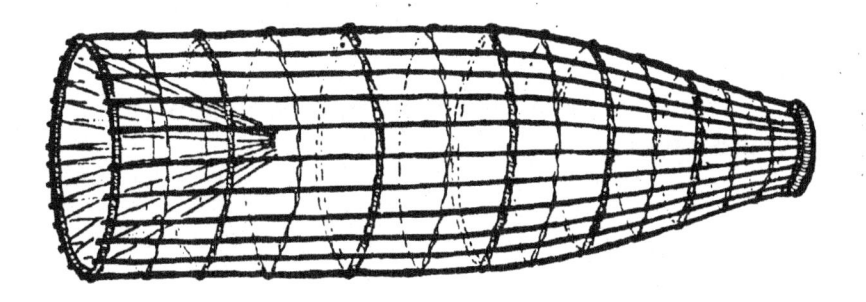

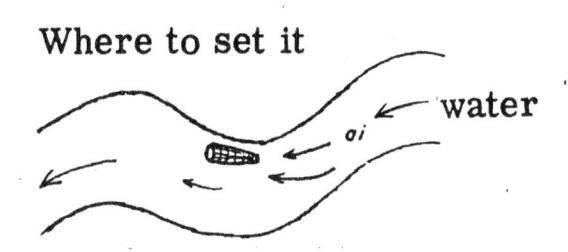

Where to set it

water

As for setting up the trap, to do it properly you lay it on a bamboo platform or floor that slants up towards the mouth of the trap, so that any fish coming to the platform will be led towards the mouth and go in.

The mouth should be half hidden and shaded with leaves and twigs so it looks inviting to the fish, and they go in and hide there. When they go in, they find they have been diddled and are trapped!

It will be better still if you take the trouble to put bait inside the trap.

The trap can be set at any time, whether the water is high or low, just as you please.

The drawing shows the trap and where it should be set.

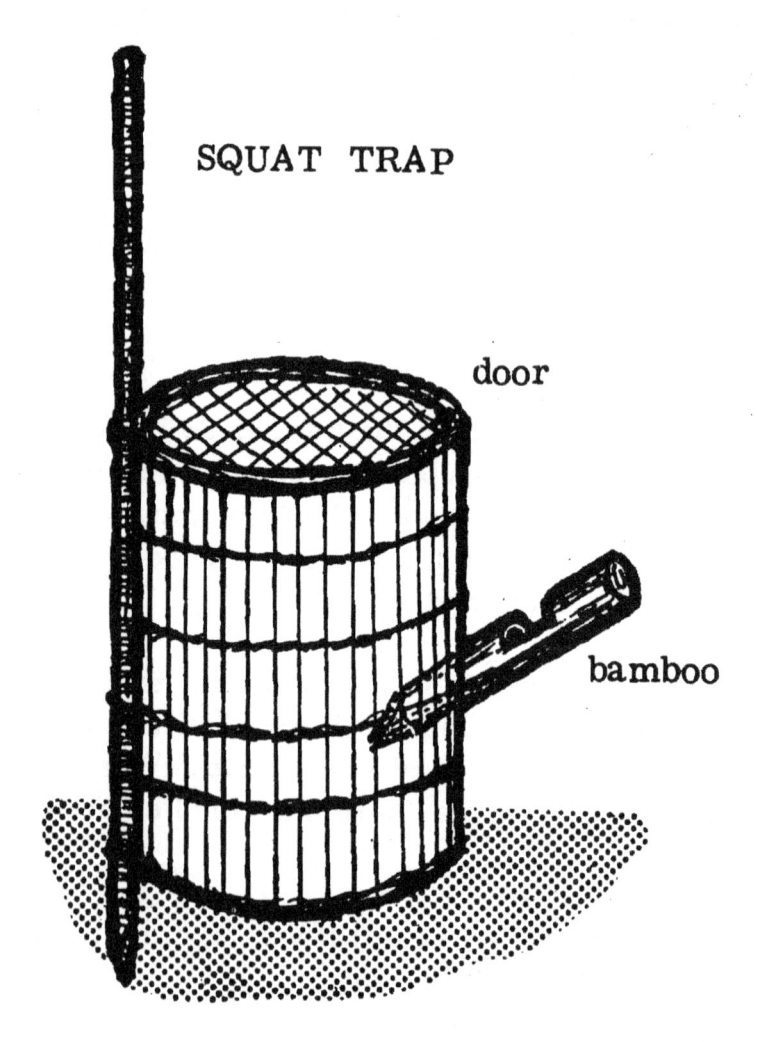

SQUAT TRAP

door

bamboo

SQUAT-TRAP

This trap is an odd-looking thing. The cone of sharp bamboo is stuck into the body of it. It will only catch small fish, such as 'enseluai'.

The cone is made on the inner end of the bamboo, and a hole is cut in the bamboo outside the trap.

The bamboo is tilted up so that when you put bits of bait in the hole they dribble down to the cone. The fish go for the bait and follow it in down the bamboo and so into the trap.

Fermented rice can be used for bait, but better than rice is an ants' nest fixed to the trap. Then the fish come after the ants and find their way into the trap.

The trap is staked down in the water, near the bank and covered with leaves and twigs, so the fish think it natural and are not disturbed by the sight of it.

The trap is called 'squat' because of its shape and the way it sits on the bottom of the water, as you can see in the drawing.

LONG NARROW-TRAP (entaya)

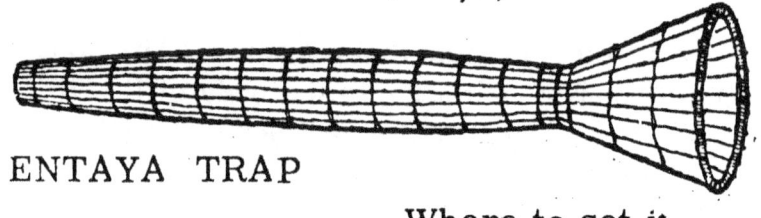

ENTAYA TRAP

Where to set it

The trap is made just like the others with bamboo and rotan and fern: but its shape is different again. Also, it is made to suit the size of the river where it is to be used, and can be up to about twelve feet long.

The long narrow-trap is set with its mouth facing up-river, not down: and in fast-running water. Don't put it in gentle water for it will catch no fish, but in fast water, the fish coming down-river will be carried into it. The drawing shows the way to set it, so that fish come down into it. You must make a fence or barrier from the mouth of it, stretching up-stream right to the banks on each side, so that the only gap left for the fish to pass is the mouth of the trap. Any bits of stick will do for the fence, fixed into the river-bed and filled up with leaves and branches to make a fish barrier.

THORN-TRAP

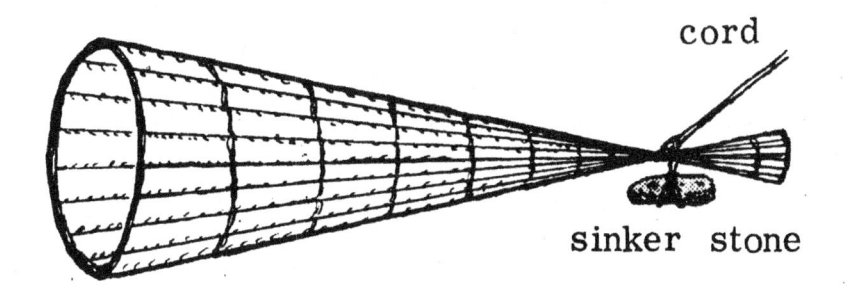

cord

sinker stone

A thorn-trap is the easiest of all to make. Hardly any work is needed for it has no inner cone as most other traps do. The thorns are the thorns of the 'maram' rotan.

Take the long thorny tips of the rotan and bind them into a cone with two or three rounds of rotan, in such a way that the thorns are all inside, pointing in from the mouth.

It should be quite small, and never bigger than your thigh. Tie a cord to the point of the cone, and tie on a stone to make it sink. Use rotan or anything handy for the cord.

For bait, use bits of leaf or anything the fish in that place are likely to eat. The fish are very choosy and have to be offered different bait at different times and in different places.

Laying the trap is as easy as can be, for there is no need to get wet and cold. All you have to do is to tie it to a branch with a cord about fifteen yards long and let the trap go into the water on the end of it.

Any fish that has scales can be taken in this trap because the scales catch on the thorns, and when a fish gets into it and is caught by the scales, it cannot get out again.

BIG TRAPS (vertical and horizontal, squatting and lying.)

Big traps are made very coarse and strong to get the big fish which will not go into a finer trap at all. So, you see, people think up all sorts of different ways of catching fish and puzzle them out till they work.

The coarse trap is made with rotan in the round, so it will be tough and strong. You must never use split rotan for this trap. The traps can be like the fence-trap, or horizontal like the log-trap, but they are shorter for their width.

The traps can be set at high water either when the river is still rising, or when it is receding, because at either time the fish will be searching about along the bank for their food. The trap should be set near the bank, where the ground juts out into the stream, and is overgrown. There is no need to bother about a platform or leading fence as you do for the other traps. These are very much easier to set: all you have to do is fix it with dead sticks and old bits of bamboo such as you will find on the spot: no hard work is needed.

However, you must shroud the mouth of it with young twigs and leaves, as for the other traps, and set a rough fence of little sticks leading towards it, so that the big fish don't see their danger and will enter in.

If you set the trap at high flood, put in bait of some sort, like rotten coconut, to bring the little fish to nibble and search for it in among the leaves and bits of driftwood. Thus you make the little fish help to trick the big ones into your trap, for when the little fish crowd round the bait, the big fellows rush up after them to eat them. Then, because the trap looks like any heap of driftwood in among bushes, the big ones run on into it and are caught.

You know as well as I do how cunning fishes are and quick to avoid danger. If we don't know the trick of it and how to fool them, we can waste a life-time making useless traps and never catch even one. For the fishes have their guardian angel too.

FINE-TRAPS

Use a fine-trap in small streams. It is no good in big rivers because the mouth is too small. Although it is made the same way as a coarse one, it takes a good deal more trouble and time to make.

When setting it, use a platform and a leading fence, as close as you can make it, and long enough to stop the fish going up-stream any other way than into your trap. Be sure to set it when the river is rising, because then the fish are moving up-stream as they feed.

Properly set, the trap will catch anything that tries to go up-stream, every kind of fish and even snakes. It should be five or six feet long, with the mouth in proportion, say about two feet across. The way of setting it is the same as for the long narrow-trap, with a leading fence, only the mouth faces down instead of up-stream.

PIPE-TRAP

Anything like bamboo or the trunk of areca palm 'pinang', can be used for a pipe-trap if it is hollow or can easily have a hole made right through. If you use bamboo, bore through all the nodes, from end to end so that it becomes a pipe.

Set it when the water is low and in hot weather, then the fish will take shelter inside it. Put it beside logs or among driftwood as if it had drifted there by itself.

When you come to lift it, stand it up on end on the bank, or in your boat, so that the water runs out at the bottom and you can take any fish that have hidden inside it.

Lift it mid-morning when the sun is getting hot, because that's the time when the fish look for shade and shelter to rest in. It's no good lifting one of these traps at night.

BOTTLE-TRAP (empuyong)

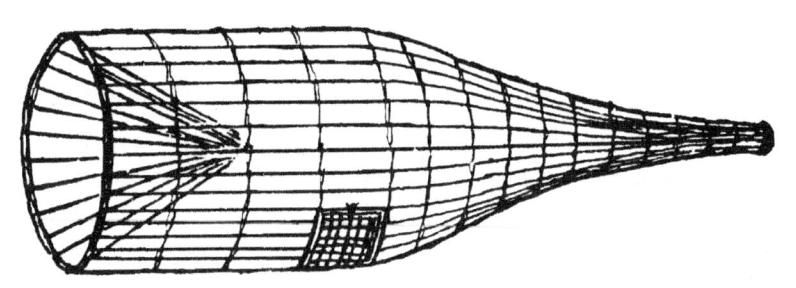

the door or lid

This is made in the same way as all the others, but it has a long neck like a bottle.

The butt-end is different from the other traps of this kind and gives it its name 'empuyong'.

The trap is tapered sharply into a snout or neck from about the middle, but the opening for getting out the fish is not in the end but in the side. It is used chiefly in places where there is shingle and fairly rapid wake. In case of a sudden rise of water, which is only too likely in such places, the trap offers less resistance to the water and there is less risk of its being swept away and lost.

When making this, or any other sort of trap that has a cone in it to prevent fish getting out again, the best bamboo or rotan to use, if you can find it, is one that has a nest of ants, wasps, or hornets on it.

Use it for the cone, because it will not break or rot so quickly. The same goes for the 'ridan' used for making fishing rods.

CHAPTER IV

BASKET-FISHING AND FISH-PONDS

BASKET-FISHING

This method is used by women to get fish from very small streams. They are not very interested in using other methods.

They make up a party to go basket-fishing. Only small fry are caught this way, of course; just tiddlers that dart about in the brooks, but with luck a few decent-sized ones are caught too.

The best time to fish with baskets is in the hot weather when the water is low, because the deeper places where they can hide are fewer: they gather together there and are not scattered all over the place.

A fishing basket can be made of all sorts of things:

'Bemban' reeds,
The bark of sago palm, cultivated or wild, and rotan.
Forest palms too, like 'gernis' (or 'gerenis').

The material is split or peeled and then woven

into a convenient shape, which is usually a long narrow basket; fairly deep, say two feet by eight inches by one foot six inches.

Often they use the milder kinds of tuba to help with the fishing, and they also collect other things while on such an expedition, such as ferns or bamboo shoots or other wild things that are good to eat.

These tiny fish are best cooked in green bamboo. The bamboo must be youngish as well as fresh cut, for then it gives a pleasant flavour to the fish, and makes it very good eating.

PONDS (see appendix C)

In many places, these days, it is getting harder to catch fish in the rivers, and it is a good idea to build a fish-pond so that you can grow your own fish, and have no need to go looking for them up and down-river.

There are more people about nowadays, and less fish to go round, so it is really essential to build fish-ponds to save time and work in getting a supply of fish when it is needed.

You can get advice from Government on how to build your pond if you are interested, and free supplies of fry to stock it with as well.

CHAPTER V
FISH POISONS AND THE WAY THEY ARE USED

There are ten different sorts of poison, all called tuba (appendix B).

'SATING'

This is a creeper with a very small leaf which grows wild in land that has been farmed: it is not cultivated though some other kinds are. It is a very strong poison indeed but the fish die slowly from it because it attacks their eyes. It first blinds them, so that they cannot see. It is most effective during hot weather.

If you use too much, it will drive even crocodiles out of the water, for they cannot stand the pain in their eyes. People usually mix it with other poisons.

There are a lot of things you must not do when using this poison. For instance, you must not speak of it as weighing so much, but you must say, "It's the size of a mousedeer", or "It's as big as a barking deer". Also, it must be pounded first, before any other poison that is being used, or it will lose its strength; people used to say long ago that its strength would be taken away by the Poison-King.

'EMPADI'

This plant is small and the root, which is the part used for poisoning fish, is a tuber rather like a 'keladi' but it is covered with small thorns and looks hairy. The poison sets up a bad itch and when you are beating out the roots you must be very careful how you speak of it. If you say it is very itchy stuff, it will itch the more.

Fish poisoned with 'empadi' flop about the river as if they are drunk.

You set about preparing it in a different way from the other kinds of tuba. You make a basket and pound it in that with a pestle about the size of your calf, or thereabouts, as is convenient to hold.

The root is wild and is never planted or cultivated. The poison is strong and if plenty of it is used it will kill the prawns and crabs as well as fish. As I said before, it makes you itch.

'KELITING'

This one has a great many restrictions and taboos connected with it and people use it very rarely because of that. There is no need, though, to have a lot of other people with you and you can use it on your own, if you like.

The plant is a creeper, thorny and thinner than your little finger. You pick the young shoots for poison and shred them with a knife, then put them between leaves and bruise them. Don't take them too old: but so young that they have no smell.

Mix them up with red ants or other ants. Many people mix in dung too, for good measure, and it works. Others use only the ants because they are not prepared to stand the smell.

You then go by boat, if the river is big, or on foot along a small stream, and put some of the poison bait into the water, stirring it about with a stick. After about a quarter of an hour the fish will come up, if you know where to put the bait and have made the right mixture.

All the time you are doing this you must swallow your spittle, and must not spit it out.

Use this poison in the early morning before anybody else is about, for that is another rule about it, made long ago. The rules must all be obeyed or the poison won't work and you will get no fish. Many have tried it, but without success, because they did not follow the proper custom.

CHILI GRASS (rumput kachang)

This is a poisonous plant, like a grass, that grows on river-banks, very handy for use in small streams when you have no other poison ready. It is not very strong and can be used safely by women and children in small brooks and rills.

It kills small fish, but does not do harm to fish of any size. Like 'sating' it attacks the eyes of the fish: it will make your eyes smart but it isn't dangerous.

You bruise it by treading it in a basket 'mansai', 'rapa', of suitable size, like the ones women use for fishing. Only very tiny fish can be poisoned this way, tiddlers in fact you might call them. They are delicious to eat if steamed in a green bamboo.

'KANTU' FRUIT

Kantu is just over the border from Lubok Antu and is the name of a people who were there before the Iban.

The poison is in the fruit, which is about the size of a rubber nut and yellowish. The plant is cultivated, because it does not grow well unless it is planted and tended. It is very much prettier than the others and could be used for decoration. The fruit can be picked up and collected from the ground, but the plant is short-lived and does not last as long as the other poison plants.

The poison attacks the stomach of the fish, which it destroys very quickly, and they die almost at once. It is, perhaps, the best of the fish poisons to use, but people very seldom trouble to plant it because it has such a short life.

People will not bring this poison to a big fish-drive, because it is too hard to get, but they make use of it when they are out on their own.

The way to use it is to put it in a small basket and pound it till it is broken up very small and the white juice comes out. Then stir it in water and pound it again till the liquid stops turning white. Use it in small streams but not in too big a river.

TREE FRUIT

The real fruit-poison comes from a fruit like a mangosteen but more egg-shaped, less rounded and of a green colour. The tree is planted, not wild, and grows to about the thickness of a gallon measure. It is light coloured and looks like a 'langgir' tree. The leaves are long.

The fruit looks edible, and the flesh of it can be eaten when fully ripe. But don't ever try to eat a green one, because the poison is in the latex of the unripe fruit.

To prepare the poison, make a wooden bowl to pound it in. Pound the fruit till it is smashed up really fine. Mix it with water, like any other poison.

Anything that lives in water will be killed by this stuff. Crabs, prawns, snails will all climb out on the bank to get away from it. The 'empelasi' fish will flip and jump right on to dry land because, of all fishes, that one takes the shortest way to safety.

Because the poison is so strong, every fish that cannot get out of the water will die, and this makes it an excellent poison to use.

SHORT CREEPER (rabut)

This looks like the ordinary poison creeper (derris), but is shorter, only growing to about five yards, and the stem is more sharply tapered.

It is collected in a different way, for you pull out roots and all and take the whole plant. If you plant it, you must plant a lot at a time or you will never have enough. It is called the "garden tuba" because it is always cultivated. It has a lot more juice than the others and so fetches a higher price when sold.

The poison can be used in any sort of stream, big or small, if you have enough of it.

The plot of ground where you plant it must be cleared and weeded pretty clean, for it doesn't do well if it's overgrown. The roots are not very long and grow close about the butt of the plant without much spreading.

This creeper is a popular kind to plant because it is easy and quick to collect, unlike the other kinds. It takes six or seven months before it is old enough to use. Chinese gardeners always keep some growing because they use the poison to keep pests off their pepper vines.

LONG GREEPER

People who live far up-river always plant this kind, because it needs no attention. Once planted, it can be left to itself until it is wanted. It is planted at the foot of a tree, so that the creeper has support to twine on and climb up.

Any time fish poison is wanted, the creeper is there for the taking.

It is hardy and long-lasting so long as too much of the root is not taken too often. One plant will weigh nearly thirty pounds, if grown in good soil and left long enough. It takes five or six years to grow to its greatest size and strength of poison, but the plants vary a good deal in the amount of juice they produce. Some plants are full of juice and some give hardly any.

TOAD CREEPER

This grows wild on the river bank, and is never planted. It is not a very strong poison.

People sometimes collect it to make up the amount they need to bring to a big fish-drive, when they haven't got enough of the stronger sort.

It looks rather like the long creeper and is sometimes mistaken for it, but it can be recognised by its rough stem: this gives it its name of "toad creeper" because it is warty, like a toad's back.

When a big crowd gathers for a fish-drive in a wide river, there will always be some who don't "play the game", and who take the lazy way of

bringing toad creeper to make up the quantity they
are supposed to bring.

POISON BARK

Poison bark is only found in the forest, growing wild. Anyone who is not at home in the forest will not be able to recognise it when they see it. It looks like the bark of the 'babai' tree, but it has a different smell. If you smell at it too much it will give you a headache.

The leaves are like those of the tree fruit-poison, but longer and narrower.

It is not a very effective poison, but it can be used when you are in the forest and can get no other. It is simply something to fall back on when you need a fish poison, and can find nothing better.

CHAPTER VI

FISH POISON: THE LAW OF THE RAJAH

Long ago there were no restrictions on people poisoning the rivers to get fish, and there was no need to get a permit. Then His Highness the Rajah saw the sad plight of the fish, and they were all killed by this means, both great and small. Small fry died to no purpose, for most were not taken up to be eaten.

Therefore, seeing the fish were in a sorry state and decreasing, slaughtered for nothing and all the small fry poisoned, (for the poison does not pick and choose, but kills anything that drinks the water it is in), the Rajah made an order that there should be less of this poisoning than before. His law set out to make longer intervals between fish-drives in any one river, so that the fish would have a chance to grow and multiply. To secure this, permission had to be sought of the Rajah's Officers for any fish-drive, and failure to seek permission beforehand led to prosecution and punishments according to the Rajah's law, and still does.

A lot of people say this law is wrong and unfair, but that is because they do not fully understand its purpose or the need for it. If they thought carefully, they would see that it would be best never to use the fish-poison at all, but that if it is to be used, then it should only be used occasionally, so that the fish have plenty of time in which to breed and grow between times.

They would see, too, that the more often a river is poisoned, the harder it will be to get any catch worth having by any other method of fishing, because the fish will be dead already of the poison. But if poison is not put in the river, the fish will multiply: there will be big ones to be caught by hook, trap or net, while the little ones will slip through nets or traps and stay alive to grow bigger in their turn. When they are big enough, they will be caught sometime or other, because people are forever after them to eat.

People will have a better time of it, not to mention the fish, because with no poisoning plenty of fish can be caught with net, trap and line. When a river is poisoned, there will be no fish to be caught there for half a year afterwards, as we all know.

CHAPTER VII

THE MANAGEMENT OF A FISH DRIVE, AND THE CUSTOMS CONNECTED WITH IT

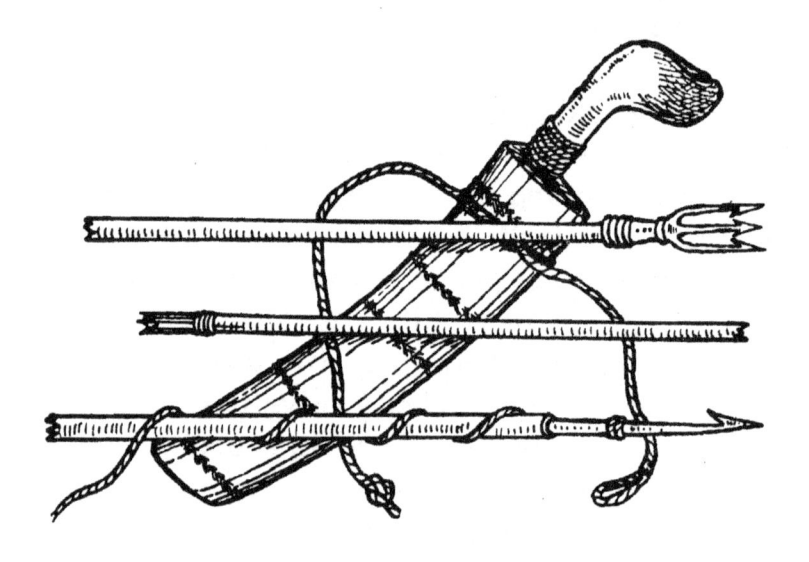

If you go to take part in a fish-drive, you should have all these things with you: A trident of three points, a harpoon of one point, a close-spear of five points in a circle, a landing net, a small dip net, and a cast net. As well as all this you need a 'parang', of course.

The leader of the drive should be one who not only knows his job but is descended from people wł have always undertaken this work, whose father and grandfather have done it before him and have passed it on.

Nowadays anyone who has had a suitable dream comes forward and claims to be a proper leader.

It is customary to have a leader for the fish-drive (whose fish-drive it is said to be), because he starts the discussions beforehand. He makes a knotted string, with a knot for each day which is to pass before the day chosen for the drive. He also decides, after discussion with the majority of those taking part, where the meeting place is to be and where the pounding of the roots is to be done.

If these things are not decided beforehand, nobody will know where to go or when.

This is for a large-scale fish-drive, in a big river, of course. There is no need to have a leader qualified by descent if a few people are fishing a small stream privately: then, anyone can make the arrangements.

In a big drive, when everybody has arrived at the place chosen, the leader will call them all to bring up their contributions of poison-creeper to one spot, so that he can see the amount. When it is all heaped together, he will wash all his amulets and charms, including all that are strong and effective for the purpose, like "Deadly

Snare", and "Destroyer". He sprinkles the heap
of roots with drops of water from the charms.

Then he utters an invocation as well as he
knows how. Great skill in this is not necessary,
but people very much like to hear it.

Part of an invocation sounds like this:-

>'O, ha! Tu ukai tubai ngapa, tubai sunga,
>Ukai bai burong, ukai bai tenong.
>Tang endang leka beri sida Laja, sida Bungai
>>Jawa,
>Bri sida Kling, bri sida Bungai Nuing.
>Ngasi, nyedi, lalu munoh meh nuan pagila
>>lusah, tulat, lupat.
>Lalu nuan, ngirau rantau, lalu nyerok lubok.
>Nyadi nuan digelar ke benama Rusa nunyau
>>rantau nyarok lubok.
>Patah tetuai, lalu patah tebiak,
>Patah ke apai, lalu patah ke indai.
>Bisa ke peregi dom tu, beji duman nuan Antu
>>Reba, Antu Rusa.
>Anang nyelingau, anang mamau,
>Tang ngeransau batang lalu ngeransau agang'.

The meaning and the sound could be given in English like this:

> Oha! Here is no weed poison, no weakling,
> Not bird-borne, nor got by divining.
> But from seed sown by Laja, seed grown by
>   Bungai Jawa.
> Brought us by Kling, boon of Bungai Nuing.
> Go hunt and slay and take your prey:
> Kill on this day and tomorrow; kill for many
>   days.
> Go ravage down the river reaches, sweeping
>   through the deeps and bays.
> You, whose name is Rusa Brookbane,
> Who is called Sambhur Pool-Pillager.
> Slay great and slay small.
> Slay fathers and mothers and children and all.
> Perish all at your passing, deadly dealer of
>   death.
> Bring dread to all them that hide among drift-
>   wood, pale ogre of pools.
> Go seep among twigs, and creep behind logs.
> Go stealthy and cold, surely and bold.

Note: Kling, Laja, Bungai Nuing and Bungai Jawa are names of heroes who lived on earth long ago.

When the prayer is made, everyone takes his own contribution of poison root and beats it to smash its skin with wooden mallets. This takes an hour or so. They then rest and have a smoke, or eat betel-nut according to their liking, but not until the leader gets up. From the start of the pounding until the time the leader gets up, nobody may smoke, or eat anything: nor may anyone mention the power of the roots to kill, for it will be a warning to the fish. It is bad luck to do any of these things, for the poison will have no effect and there will be no fish caught. This is called 'jelungan', for which a fine is payable.

The leader must be the first to move down-river too, after the poison has been put in. Then he reaches out and takes up a fish and he casts it towards the setting of the sun, so that all the fish may droop and die.

That done, he shouts aloud so that all may hear and follow. Then, and not before, everybody gets going and races as fast as they can after any fish that comes to the surface poisoned.

There are very many customs and taboos connected with poisoning fish. If a drive does not kill many fish, or there is a minor fault, 'jelungan'; some of the people will pound more roots, "to kill more of the fish", as they say. This is done also where the river is tidal: the first lot is put in an hour or two before the end of the ebb and a second lot, freshly prepared, is put in as the tide turns, which is followed up-river.

If you see a fish beside someone else's boat, you must not strike at it with your spear carelessly or unless it is beyond the bows of your own boat. And never throw your spear and let go of it, or you may hurt someone badly.

At a good distance down-river from the starting point, people make a barrier of bamboos or nets so that the fish cannot escape that way. They put coarse seine-nets, or a log-trap, or a stake-net in the water, so that the fish will enter in and be caught as they try to escape from the poison. Some log-traps are also set up-river in case any fish succeed in avoiding the poison in that direction.

It would take far too long to set out all the details of fishing with poison, but this is the main part of it, set down in a very few words.

HUNTING ON LAND

A description of various methods of hunting animals which are used in the Rejang.

CHAPTER VIII

DO'S AND DON'TS WITH A GUN

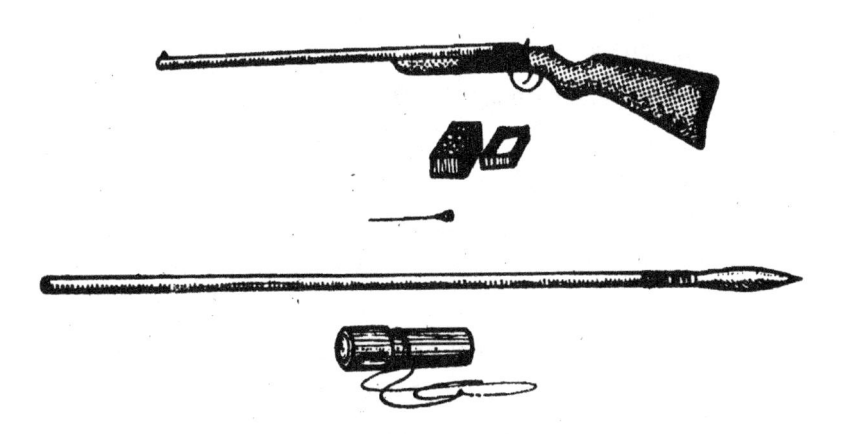

You have to be careful in all sorts of ways when you go out shooting. If you don't go out very far you mustn't stand unwary in one place for long, or move carelessly, for fear that someone else coming that way on the same errand may take you for a deer or a pig, and fill you full of buckshot.

In the same way when you are moving yourself you must be both alert and cautious, and not blaze away at anything that moves or cracks a twig or shakes a branch. If you don't get a fair sight of all your target, don't fire. If you can only see part of something and can't be quite sure what it is, wait till you can be. Too many people are hasty and fire too soon.

Keep your wits about you and use your eyes and ears all the time. If you only get a glimpse of something and let yourself be led into rash firing by your keenness to get game, you may easily imagine it is an animal when it is really a man, and shoot him by mistake.

You should not have accidents when carrying a gun in the forest if you are very careful to keep a watch on yourself as well as other people.

If you hear a slight sound, stop and stand still. Look about you in every direction without hurry. Don't be careless, and don't let yourself be surprised or startled into a wrong movement. Keep your nerves steady: if you don't keep calm, you are much more likely to do something foolish. If you keep a firm grip on yourself and stay calm and collected, you will be successful in doing what everyone tries to do to gain strength, and your hunting will be good.

Watch out near very big trees when you are after game in the forest; there may be a python or something hiding there. When you are sure there is nothing, you can pass by without risk and carry on the hunt. Go cautiously near any big tree, whether it standing or fallen, or lying rotted upon the ground.

If you do not know these things and cannot take enough care there is no use in going into the forest. You will only tire yourself out and gain nothing, the labour will be in vain and quite meaningless.

HOW TO HANDLE A GUN

A police officer has been good enough to give us some hints on how to handle and use a shotgun. He gives reasons why there is need for more care on the part of many people:-

Every year people die of gunshot wounds: some are shot by friends or neighbours, some have accidents with their own guns. The law provides that people who are convicted of hurting or killing others by careless use of firearms shall be punished by fine or imprisonment. Shooting someone on purpose is of course murder and can be punished with death. In any case, there is a customary fine to be paid to the relatives of the person killed, which may amount to five hundred dollars.

Carelessness can bring sorrow that is not helped by punishments: friends, brothers or children can be killed, or one's own father. But if the advice given below is scrupulously followed there need be no accidents at all.

1. Always 'break' the gun to see that it isn't loaded, before carrying it.

2. Don't point a gun at anyone at any time. This is foolish.

3. See that your gun is unloaded before going up into a house or getting into a boat.

4. Be careful how you carry a gun as you walk. If it is loaded, carry it pointed upwards. If it is not loaded, 'break' it and carry it in the crook of your elbow ready to load.

5. Never hand a loaded gun to anyone else. Never lay a loaded gun on the ground, or leaning against a tree, or stowed in a boat. 'Break' it first and see it is unloaded.

6. Only load the gun shortly before you need to fire it. Don't hurry. When you turn for home, 'break' it and unload.

7. Don't shoot at anything near a pathway. The law forbids shooting within 100 yards of a road or path commonly used.

8. Be careful how you shoot in thick country. Look well and don't fire until you can be quite sure what it is you are aiming at. Carelessness over this causes many deaths: friends are mistaken for pigs.

9. Never go hunting with other people, unless one of you is put in command. Obey his orders. If you are told to watch in a certain place, stay there and don't wander about.

10. If a deer, or pig, comes into view between you and someone else, never fire at it. It has so often happened that the other man gets shot and the deer or pig is missed.

If you remember these points and make a habit of obeying them, you will not have accidents. If you don't bother with them there will certainly be more wounds and deaths; the one who shoots the other may be imprisoned for years, and fined, and his gun forfeited. Both families concerned will suffer for one man's carelessness.

CHAPTER IX

HUNTING

If you go hunting in the forest for any kind of game, be very careful. And be careful and patient all the time, because it is a long job and may take all day: it's not an occupation for an hour or two.

If you are out early in the morning, go by the foot of the hills because the pig and deer will still be lying there. But by mid-day, they hide themselves behind ridges and hills in dense undergrowth because they think that men will not be bothered to go looking in tangled and precipitous places.

And so, if you go upon the land and seek in such places, you will certainly find them if there are any there at all.

When you walk in the forest, don't use your heels and don't go flat footed, lift your heels and go on tip-toe softly so as not to be heard by the beasts you are hunting. The need to walk so quietly can easily be proved: put an ear down touching the ground and rest your cheek on the earth; then get someone else to walk nearby in a normal fashion. You will be surprised how loudly you can hear him pound the earth every time he puts a foot down. That is why the pig and the deer always put their heads to the ground from time to time as they go about looking for food, so that they can hear anything coming that is likely to disturb or harm them. I've watched them do it myself.

Another thing to remember in the forest is to be very careful where you walk. Use your eyes and ears as well as experience, especially because of pythons which are the most likely to attack you. They don't go for you because they are man-eaters but because they think you are simply a sort of animal they can eat. So don't go too close to the buttresses of big trees, or big fallen trees and logs, because that's where they lie in ambush. It is only in such places that people do get attacked by them.

Don't be careless or thoughtless in the forest, and don't day-dream, for you never know when you may run into danger. Other animals lie in wait to get their food too, and are always on the watch to protect themselves by attack rather than flight. So never go without a 'parang' and a small knife. And if a python attacks you, you must hold hard to a tree or creeper - and be quick about it so that you too have a purchase and can't be dragged about.

If you want to go hunting deer or pig in daylight, you must choose a piece of country where you know they usually live, and you must choose the weather. The best time is when it has been hot all day except for a good shower of rain in the early afternoon. If the sun has come out again after rain, say about three hours before dark, that will be the time to go and stalk them. They will have been cold and shivering in the rain and will take the chance to get dry and warm again.

If there is any game of this sort about then you will surely find it if you look in the more open places where the sunlight strikes through.

SHOOTING NEAR A SALT-LICK

If you are after 'rusa' deer at a place they often use, or at a salt-lick you have prepared and which you know they come to, first build a good strong platform and put walling round it so that you can see without being seen. You must watch from here at night.

You must be careful where you put the hut. See which way the wind usually blows and put the hut down-wind from the salt-lick, so that the deer will not pick up your scent. If it is wrongly placed you will waste nights in watching and come home with nothing to show for your efforts but a haggard face and drooping eyelids.

A lot of people who use this method lie in wait at the salt-lick and get nothing, or very little, because the beasts take fright. If only one of them scents the hunter he will be startled and run off: then the others will be afraid and run off too.

If you want to hunt this way, it's best to wait beside a game track leading to the bait, but not close in. About five hundred yards off is a fair distance, so that you can get a shot in while your pig or deer is still travelling and before he gets cautious, close to the bait. If you fire a shot in a place that far off you can move round to another spot and have another go, which you can't do if you are too close in. The chances are that game on other tracks will not have heard your shot or, if they have, so faintly as not to matter.

Also, if you bring down one of them, no other game will come that way as long as the blood remains on the ground, because they are much more canny than we are at seeing to their own safety. The ones we get are only those whose number is up, like a man for whom the doctors can do no more.

When choosing a place to lie in wait, don't tread on the game tracks at all, because pig and deer have noses a lot keener than their eyes with

which to find us. Their sharpest sense is that of
smell, then hearing, then sight. That is why you
should also find out which way the wind is blowing:
if it blows from them to you it will be all right,
but if it carries your scent to them you will find
it hard indeed to get one of them. If the wind is
too gentle for you to tell its direction by feeling
it, scrape a finger nail with a knife and see which
way the dust goes. Then you can take up a position where you will not scare the beasts and you
have a good chance of getting one.

The deer always visit the salt-lick most at the
new moon. Therefore, during the moon's first
quarter is the best time to hunt at night. Not only
deer, but all kinds of animals are moving about
pretty freely at that time.

HUNTING BY PLANTATIONS (Shooting in tapioca
plots)

When you have tapioca planted and need to
protect it, and so preserve it as food for yourself,
the usual way is to make a hut on a platform near
the growing crop. The platform must not be too
far off or the shot will not bring down the game:
as far as the shot will fairly reach is good enough.

In the case of pig, however, it is better to be
a good way off from the crop itself so that they are

not suspicious. Seek out the path they use and watch that, taking care that the wind is right and you are not placed so that your scent can be carried to them and so warn them of danger.

The pig, in particular, is cunning, even more so than we are, so you must plan very carefully indeed when you set out to get him. He always moves very cautiously and takes great care when he goes after tapioca or anything else planted by man that he likes to eat. He knows very well who it belongs to, and that the owner may be on the lookout for thieves.

When hunting pig or deer in these places, you must never walk along their track; never even tread on it, or you will spoil your chances. For they will find your scent if you have walked in their tracks and they will make off at once. To avoid scaring them and turning them back, you must give any tracks you see as wide a berth as you can. Once scared off they will not come that way again.

And never forget the weather either. If it is a stormy day, the stalking will be very long and hard and most likely without success. If it is a fine day, then you can expect some luck because they will be bolder to move about when everything is quiet under a hot sun. If the weather is bad with much rain and wind, all the trees will be creaking and the leaves rattling and they will be afraid of every sound, thinking that men are after them. When it is stormy all the beasts of the forest stay close and will not move about because it is their nature to be wild and fearful.

HUNTING WITH HOUNDS

Hunting with hounds is difficult and dangerous if there is no proper discussion of a plan of action beforehand by all those who are joining in. There must be full discussion beforehand and agreement as to what each hunter is to do, so that everyone knows what is afoot and understands the part he has to play. Only then can you go out to the agreed place for starting and begin the hunt.

Never, never follow hounds too closely when they are giving tongue, or you will run into trouble as sure as the river runs into the sea.

If you run too hard you will grow excited and forget all about what was agreed on before you started.

Whoever is setting the hounds on must not get too close or rush in upon them, for fear that someone lying in wait may take him for the pig. But there will be no accidents if everything is agreed, and understood, before the hunt is begun.

In the same way, when hunting with a gun, if you come upon a thicket or any place that is full of undergrowth and hard to get through, you must say something. It doesn't matter what you say so long as anybody else who may be there will know that you only have two legs, and won't take a pot shot at you.

People who use hounds regularly for hunting look after them well and train them to answer to their names as well as obey various other calls. Examples of names are Nganit, Garam, Busau, Nyeling: and modern ones may be Corporal, or Bandit.

HUNTING MIGRATING PIG

The bearded wild pig migrates in March and sometimes in October. In the Rejang they come from the 'ulu' Mukah southwards and cross the river, eating fallen fruit and damaging crops as they go. They are sometimes shot and left as vermin when they are too numerous. I have known them travel thirty and forty at a time and have heard Ibans complain they have been seen with wreaths of padi on their heads. A few cross the Rejang as far down as Song but very many cross the river near the Pelagus rapids and that is a favourite place to wait for them. They never seem to move back north; at least, not in noticeable numbers.

At one time they must have migrated over a wider area. There is a legend told at Kanowit concerning Siong of Pasai, son of the hero Tugau, and these wild pig. It maintains that the pig were transformed humans (or vice versa), and Siong married one of them, only to become a widower when she was killed on one of their fruit-hunting forays across river.

The pig are easiest to take as they swim a river. But don't wait on the side where they come down to the water: they will scent you and turn back inland. So keep away on the other side, the side where they land and climb ashore. Keep under the trees and ready in your boat so that when the pig are half way across you can go for them and get more of them.

Never take a gun on a hunt for swimming pig. Too many people have been shot and killed while racing for the pig in mid-river. Also, as when using fish poison, never throw a spear, harpoon or trident, for fear you might hurt someone else in the excitement.

If you use a light racing-boat for this, like a fifteen-man boat, it will be too slow in turning because of its length. But a light boat for six or eight men is handier and much easier to turn smartly in any direction. You will find that people using short boats get far more pig than those who go in for very long or heavy boats; when there are a lot of pig on the move, that is.

When you spear a pig in the water, don't strike it in the belly, or it will sink before you can secure it. The best place is across the backbone, in the saddle, but not too hard or too deep; then it will be easy to capture him and get him onto the steep bank. But again, if you strike too hard and cut too deep, he will sink like a stone and you will lose him.

CHAPTER X

NETS AND TRAPPING

NETS

Some people are very clever at making and using nets to catch pig or deer. The nets are not long, only about three yards; they can be made of rope the size of a little finger and should be stained or darkened by tanning. The edge is fitted with a running noose.

The net is set up across a track used by the animals, and is held in position by tying loosely to trees or five foot sticks stuck in the ground. The standing part of the noose is made fast to a tree beside the track.

The game is then driven. It will follow the track and rush into the net, the ties will part and the noose will close the net like a bag with the animal inside.

The odd thing is that either pig or deer go limp as soon as they are in the net and lie down quietly without struggling. They seem to tire all at once and so are very easy to take.

The net is called 'badal' but it is very rarely seen these days.

NOOSE-NETS FOR DEER (jarin)

These are made of rotan in the round, and not split. They consist of a series of nooses each about four feet across attached to a heavy plaited line at intervals of about two feet so that they overlap. The line with its nooses is made as long as possible but not more than can be carried by one man. Several of these may be used at one time. (See cover illustration.)

The nets are set across the deer tracks with the nooses hanging from the line and almost touching the ground. Then the deer are driven with hounds, or simply by beaters using their voices. As the deer run in fear trying to escape, they run into the nets and draw the nooses tight on themselves.

There must be a good steady man chosen to keep watch at the nets, one who will not get excited and rush in as soon as a deer has been caught. He must keep clear of the nets and be careful how he approaches when a deer is caught, or he may get snarled up in the nooses himself. It has been known for people to lose their lives by getting tangled in the nets when racing one another to be first at the kill.

There is a lot of work in making these nets and a lot more in using them. They are heavy and have to be carried out and back again each time they are used. People hardly ever use them now, because they have shotguns. The Malays used them a great deal at one time, but not much now because there are far fewer deer about. It is great sport to catch deer in this way because they are caught alive: they can be kept alive and tamed if caught young enough.

The Saribas Malays call a bicycle a 'jarin' vehicle because it looks like a noose-net from the side and acts in the same way if you run into one in a busy street.

SPRING-TRAPS

Another way of getting deer and pig is by setting spring-traps. But spring-traps can be very dangerous both to other people and to those who set them. People who set them can forget exactly where they put them, and run into their own traps; the neighbours are even more likely to get caught if they don't know traps have been set. Such traps should not be used by people who are careless and forgetful, or by very old people. A very old man may wander about and may even forget he has set any traps. If the trap is not clearly marked by warning signs and if everyone in the longhouse and, in fact, everyone who is likely to go that way is not told where the traps are set, they may easily walk into one and be badly hurt or even killed.

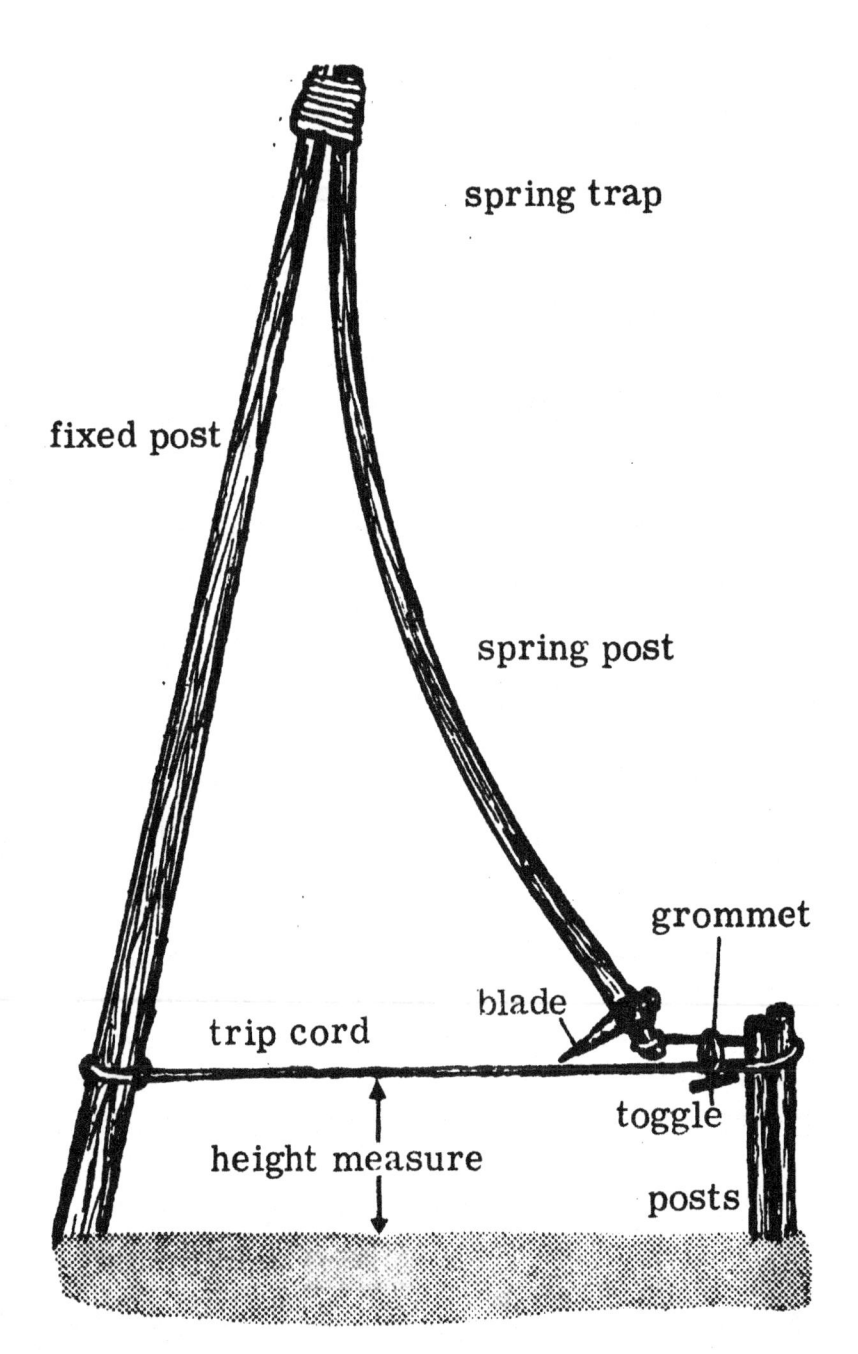

spring trap

fixed post

spring post

grommet

blade

trip cord

toggle

height measure

posts

A good place to put spring-traps is at the edge of a padi field, to protect it. You might have to, if you haven't the wherewithal to buy a shotgun. But the traps should be set right at the edge of the field, as part of the fence put to keep animals out. The usual warning marks should be set up some little way off in the forest so that anyone from another longhouse who has missed his way and comes to the farm will not get hurt by your traps. At least, he won't if he keeps his eyes open.

The sign is made by slicing downwards into a tree and fixing a sliver of wood cross the slit so made. The white sliver can easily be seen. The sign should be put at the side of a well-used path where it will be seen. The trigger part of the trap can be left visible to show exactly where the trap is. Anyone who sees the sign will understand and be warned because it has always been used from long ago.

As well as putting up the marks, you must tell everyone who is farming nearby and everyone who uses that bit of country, so that they will know what you are doing and will be on the look-out for the warning marks as they go about their business.

A measuring stick 'tuntun' is used to set the trip-cord at the proper height. The stick is marked for the length of your own fore-arm, from elbow to

TRIGGER FOR SPRING TRAP

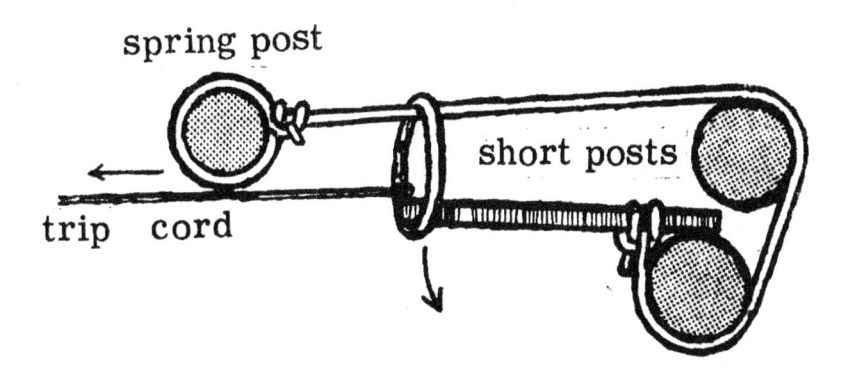

spring post

trip cord

short posts

OLD FASHIONED TRIGGER

spring post

trip cord

short post

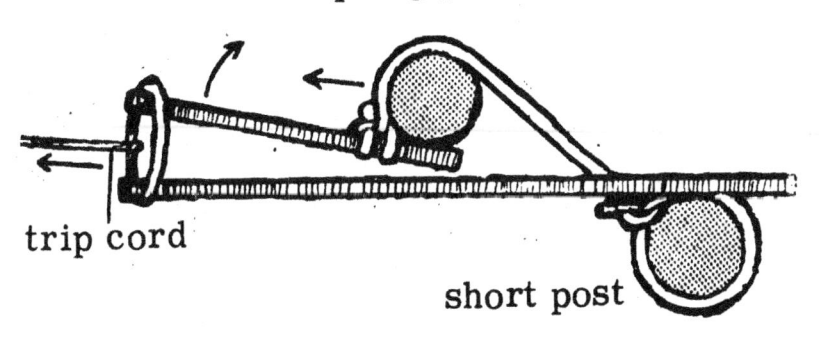

tip of extended middle-finger. Above the mark is the head of the stick, about a finger's length, often handsomely carved to represent a forest spirit but always at least notched for eyes and mouth. The head of one from the Undup is shown on the cover of this book: it is made of 'belian' and the figure has been given eyes of white bone.

The mark of fore-arm length is used for pig and the total length for deer when the stick is stood upon the ground.

On one occasion after several unsuccessful attempts to find out if these traps were much used I asked an old man in another house. His reply was, "Yes, I'm always setting traps but have no luck. The pig take all my tapioca, whatever I do." When I asked to see his measuring stick, he said, "Help yourself   There's three or four in that basket. I've borrowed other people's sticks to see if they're better than mine, but they don't seem to be."

Another kind of spring trap is called the Hurler. It is very dangerous because it can't be seen at all: it is built low and as much as ten feet from the track. The trip-cord is very long. Instead of striking with a fixed blade, it hurls a spear just above the trip-cord, working horizontally.

HURLER TRAP

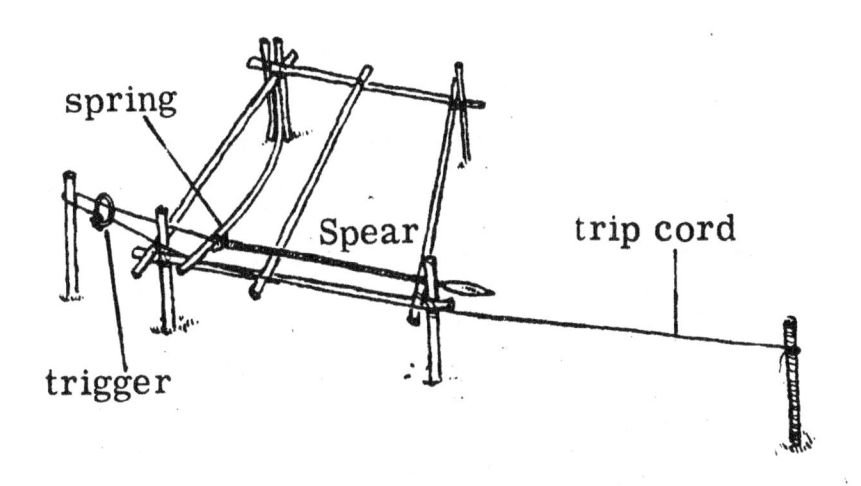

spring

Spear

trip cord

trigger

Some people set these traps to fire shotguns instead of casting spears and then they are more dangerous than ever. The authorities don't know it's done and it is always kept a close secret. People really know it's wrong to take such absurd risks: and they know too that they are likely to be more severely dealt with if anyone gets hurt.

The Traps Order made by H.H. the Rajah laid down that people could be fined and made to pay compensation for injuries caused by their traps, particularly if they had not given notice nor issued warnings enough.

A trap set for pig will smash the knee, one set for a deer will drive the hardened bamboo blade through a man's thigh.

NOOSE AND BASKET-TRAPS

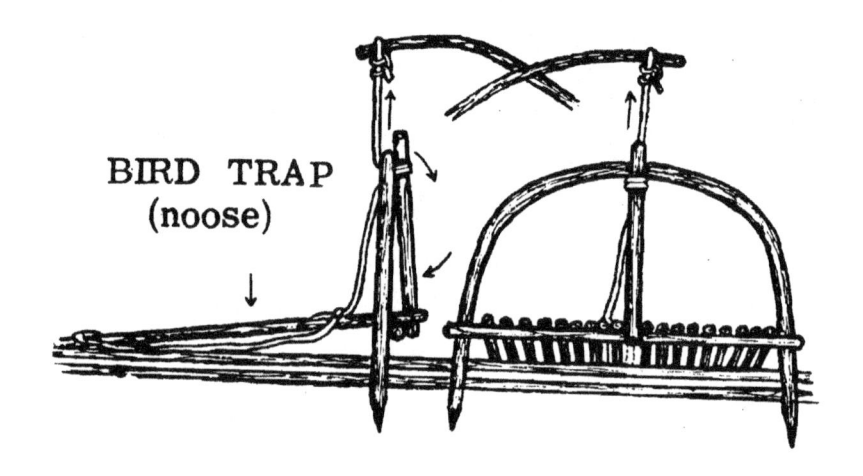

BIRD TRAP (noose)

These are similar, with triggers that either spring a noose, or let fall a basket. They need bait but are useful for catching pigeons and other ground birds in fairly open ground.

THE GHOST'S DOORWAY

There is another trap which is most effective in forest and simple to make. People in the Lemanak call it the 'Bugau' Trap or the Ghost's Doorway, because nothing gets through but a spirit. (Bugau is the name of a people living in the middle Kapuas.

GHOST'S DOORWAY

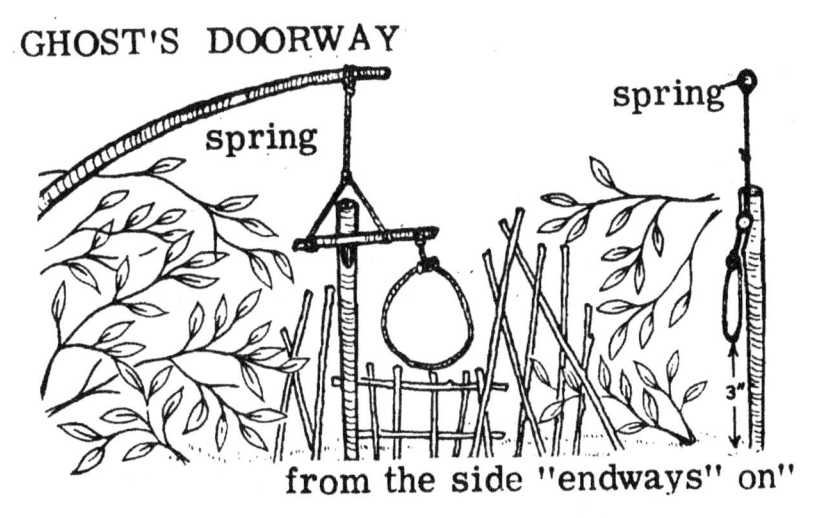

spring ... *spring*

from the side "endways" on

There is no need for a gun and the trap is in no way dangerous to human beings because it is low on the ground and small. The trap will catch any small thing that goes upon the ground in the forest, mousedeer, snakes, and ground feeding birds like the fire-back pheasants, 'sempidan', and green wood partridges, 'sengayan'.

First of all you need fine cords. The bark fibre of the 'pendok' tree, or any similar material that can quickly be rolled into a strong cord will do. The cord should be as fine as the lead of a pencil and each piece need only be long enough to make a noose three or four inches across, say half a span. You will need more of the bark in rather longer lengths to tie the trigger piece to the spring stick, but they need only be in strips and not rolled into cord.

There are right and wrong ways of taking the bark. If you tug it off the tree anyhow you will have to waste time stripping the inner fibre from the outer bark. When a downward slit is cut in the bark, bend the end right over on itself and then draw it down against the tree slowly: the continuous folding of the bark as it is stripped off the tree separates out the fibre you want to use.

Then get twigs to make a fence each side of the noose, a stout stick for the notched holding post and a long one for the spring rod. The last can be of any wood that is springy and does not remain bent when it is hauled down to set the trap.

When you go to set the traps you must first look for the little paths made by the game on the forest floor. You will find they go east and west because the game nearly always moves with the sun when feeding and hardly ever north and south across the rays of the sun.

This means that the line of traps must lie north and south across all the game paths. Cut leafy branches and small bushes and lay them without gaps all along the line you have chosen. Lay them down; there is no need to stick them in the ground and there is no need to lay them where there is a very big tree, for the animals avoid the dangers of big trees as we do.

Then set the noose traps in this rough fence, six to ten yards apart and in the game tracks as often as you can. It does not take long to set a line of twenty or thirty traps, two or three hundred yards long. Then you go home and leave them till morning.

It is best to be out early next morning to look at the traps because anything caught will be killed by the noose and may be taken, or go bad, by the time you get there if you are late.

Don't walk closer to the traps than you need and don't touch them unless they need adjusting or there is something caught and you have to reset the trap. This will allow your scent to fade from the traps and game will come closer. Traps three days old will catch far more than when they are freshly made.

The animals and birds are creatures of habit and will always try to go a known way. If they suspect something wrong or unusual, they will be very cautious and keep clear for a time. When they are satisfied, and there has been no movement or sound to upset them for a long while, they will go on along their ways and into the gap where the noose is. They will not go past the fresh cut bushes and leaves that are lying in an unnatural way and they will not go near the bole of a big tree. They can hardly see the noose at all because the fresh bark darkens very quickly and their eyes are less sharp than their noses or ears; also they will be moving at night. The little gateway seems to them to be the only way they can go and they are suddenly snatched up into the air.

CHAPTER II

OTHER METHODS OF HUNTING

DEER-HOOKS

People do not make much use of deer-nets or box-traps because of the labour involved, but we are told that it is possible to catch deer in traps armed with hooks or nooses, set at salt-licks. The bait is salt in an empty salt sack or something of the kind. The deer will lick at the salt and spring the trap. The hook must be very big and heavy to hold them when it catches in their mouths, and the nooses must be heavy too.

LAMPLIGHT

Some people take a lamp with a reflector to go hunting at night. On land they use a shotgun and on the water, for fish, a trident. In the Rejang when the fish are all going up-river to spawn everybody goes out in boats with a lamp of some sort to spear the fish. At that time the fish are swimming close enough to the surface to make a streak in the water that you can see with any light, however weak. A strong light will confuse them and they will swim towards it.

The lamp most commonly used is a brass kerosene lamp, with a narrow chimney and a handle to hold it by. A brass reflector fits over the chimney which is covered with a net of fine wire twisted upon it. If the chimney cracks, then it will not fall to pieces and let the lamp blow out.

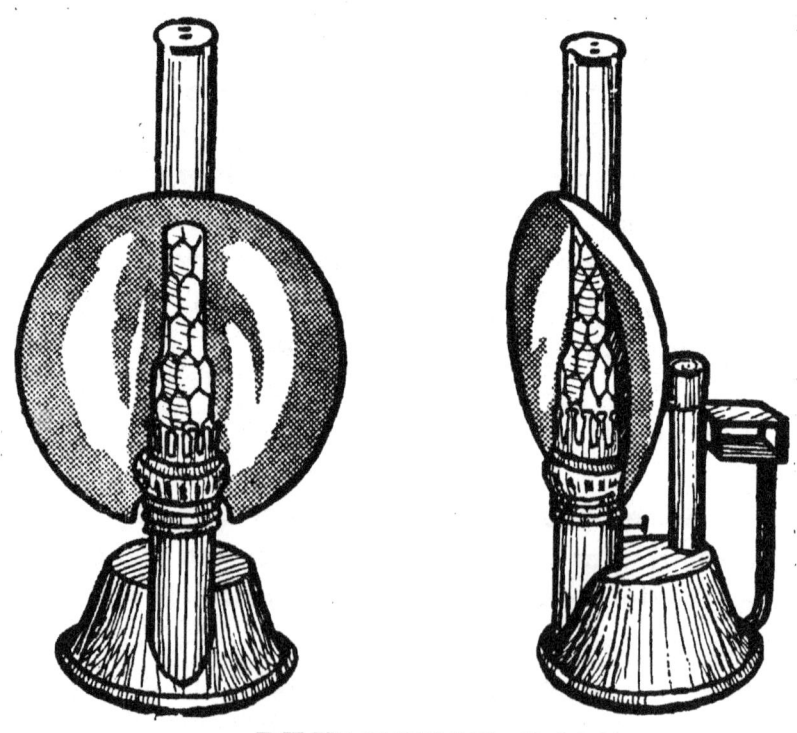

REFLECTOR LAMP

It is possible to get powerful acetylene lamps, and lamps worked by batteries these days, but the latter are heavy and the former are very hot and full of dangerous gas. The brass lamps are cheap and light, and throw a very good beam if the reflector is properly polished.

If you are out on business of your own and see someone hunting with a lamp, it will show you up clearly at a hundred yards or more. If you spot him early enough, go into hiding till he has passed, or, if you cannot do that, call out and make yourself known. Never behave like a deer and stare at the light in surprise, for your eyes will show at the right height and you will probably get shot.

MAY-FLIES

Mention should be made too of the white mayflies swarming. They fall on the water and die, particularly in the broad reaches below Kanowit in May, so that the river is almost all white with them. The fish come up to feast, and can be caught with spears by daylight, but you have to be very quick to spot your fish when he comes within reach.

LIMING

Latex of the 'pedalai' tree is mixed with other latex and cooked in a pan. The sticky mixture is then spread on small sticks which are set in places where birds often alight or small animals move, such as at the edge of a gravel bank by the water. This method is often used in padi-farms to help protect them by catching munias 'pipits', and Malay lorikeets, 'entelit'.

CALLING

The Kayans make a bamboo pipe to imitate the sound of a pigeon and sound it from inside a little leafy hut where they hide. Pigeons attracted by the call can be grabbed as they go into the hut. Some people are also able to call the barking deer.

BLOW PIPES AND POISONED DARTS

The making of these is not described because we do not know it in detail and because people who still use them are not likely to read what we write. It is said that the blowpipe is better in one way than the shotgun: it makes no noise. The bang of a shotgun startles everything within hearing so you don't get a second shot: but a blowpipe dart flies with no sound and, if you miss with one, you can try again at the same target. You have to be able to go quietly and get pretty close, because a blowpipe dart does not carry so far, nor has it the spread of a shotgun cartridge.

BOX-TRAPS

These are used for deer and are very like the box-trap for fish but bigger. The main difference is in the trigger that lets down the door. The fish-trap has a trigger like the one used for a spring-trap set high up, while the trigger for the deer-trap can be as illustrated and set in the ground nearby.

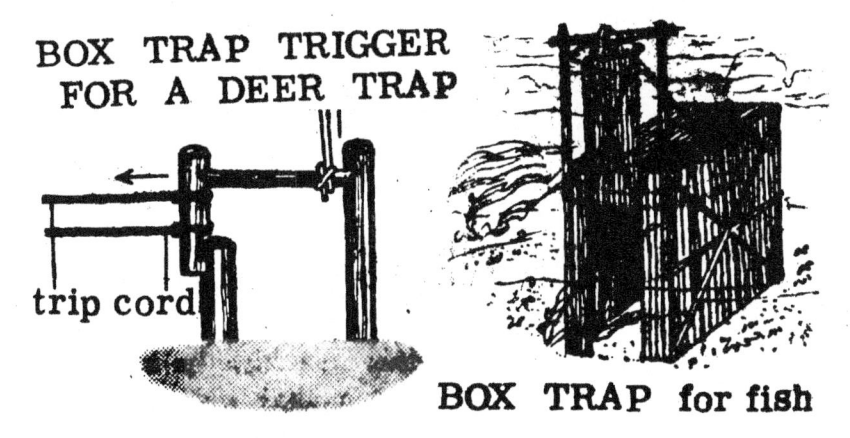

BOX TRAP TRIGGER FOR A DEER TRAP

trip cord

BOX TRAP for fish

People in the Batang Ai use these traps for fish a great deal but in the Rejang they are chiefly used by the Foochows near Sibu. The trouble with these traps is that they need careful building, but can be destroyed very quickly by floating timber in time of flood.

Another kind of box-trap is made with smooth walls of bark extending about six feet above a low fence but open at the top. Springy sticks are set to stretch out across the top. Bait of some kind, often ripe fruit, is put on the ground inside and can be seen through the fence from the ground, or from on top. Monkeys and other small climbing animals will bend down the sticks with their own weight to get at the bait: the sticks fly up again and the monkeys cannot climb the smooth walls to get out.

BOX TRAP for monkeys etc.,

CRUSHER-TRAPS

These are similar to the last, but can be set on a branch or a log, and rely on a heavy piece of wood to fall and pin down the animal that runs there and springs the trap. They are often used to kill squirrels. There is also a small box-trap which is set on logs where squirrels run and has a falling door like the bigger box-traps.

CHAPTER XII

WAYS OF COOKING WHAT YOU CATCH

The women prepare fish and meat in many ways. Here are some of them: -

Stewing in green bamboo. With leaves for flavouring, 'daun tubu, daun pait'.

Boiling after wrapping in leaves.

Roasting

Boiling

Smoking - hang above a fire for two or three days until dry and cooked.

Salting - mix with salt and place in a small jar, sprinkling more salt over the top.

Parboiling - for fish: boil until half cooked, then drain and rub with salt. Wrap it in a flower-spathe of betel nut, or palm leaf, and keep it in the rack over the fireplace. Any suitable leaf wrapping will do.

APPENDIX A

FRUITS AND BERRIES SUITABLE FOR BAIT

Iban	Scientific Name
Ara Kali	Ficus sp.
Belati	Microcos sp.
Bungkang	Aglaia odoratissima, also Eugenia.
Dabai	Canarium odontophyllum
Dadak	Artocarpus dadah
Empili	Quercus and Lithocarpus spp.
Engkabang	Shorea gysbertsiana (Illipe)
Engkala	Litsaea resinosa
Engkuang	Dracontomelum mangiferum
Ensurai	Dipterocarpus oblongifolius
Getah	Hevea brasiliensis and Sapotaceae (rubber)
Jabang	Manihot utilissima (tapioca-root)
Jambu ai	Eugenia spp. (and the flowers)
Kari	Ficus spp.
Kasai	Pometia pinnata
Kemali	Croton sp.
Kepapa	Vitex spp.
Pitoh	Swintonia acuta
Tegelam	Shorea seminis.

APPENDIX B

FISH POISONS.

The following notes on species of tuba are the preliminary results of a study being undertaken by Mr. B.E. Smythies.

Species of tuba

A. Derris Species

Derris is a genus of woody climbers and small trees of the family Leguminosae, found in the tropics generally. Several of the genus are fish-poisons, both in Asia and in South America. At least five species are planted by Ibans and used under the following names:-

Iban	Latin
1. T. akar or T. randau or T. semblawi.	D. malaccensis, Prain.
2. T. akar, or T. china or T. kebun.	D. elegans, Benth.
3. T. rabut	D. thyrsiflora, Benth.

4. T. raras, T. amat .. .. .. D. elliptica, Benth.

5. T. raung .. .. D. trifoliata, Lour.
    (syn. D. uliginosa, Benth.)

T. 'china' or T. 'kebun', is identified by watery sap and by the pinkish tubers, which have to be burnt before use. A tentative key based on characters of leaf and habit follows, but this can be improved by further study in the field.

Tentative key to the Sarawak species of Derris (tuba).

Either 1. Leaflets 3 - 7

    (a) Leaflets 3-5; midrib usually sharp on upper surface. Riversides. D. trifoliata, Lour. syn. D. uliginosa, Benth.

    (b) Leaflets 5-9. Midrib sunken above.

    (c) Leaflets 5-7; very thin, completely glabrous, with reddish nerves; margins not inrolled. Small climber or bush, only thrives in open places. D. thyrsiflora, Benth.

(d) Leaflets 7-9; rather thin, tending to be whitish on undersurface; nerves pale; large climber, planted in temuda and left to grow in secondary forest. D. malaccensis, Prain.

Or 2 Leaflets 9-13; tall climbers grown in secondary forest.

(e) Leaves and stem entirely glabrous, without pale undersurface; leaflets very thin, without inrolled margins; nerves reddish. D. elliptica, Benth.

(f) Leaves and stem more or less hairy when young, leaflets whitish beneath when young; margins tending to be inrolled.

(g) Leaflets 9-13. Young leaflets coarsely and densely hairy beneath. D. elegans, Benth.

(h) Leaflets 7-9; young leaflets sparsely hairy beneath, along midrib and main veins. D. malaccensis, Prain.

B. Non-derris species of tuba.

1. T. 'buah'   Diospyros spp.

A rather large genus of trees and shrubs of the family Ebenaceae, found throughout the tropics, and best known for the ebony wood obtained from some species.

The fruits of the following Bornean species are used as fish poison:-

D. lanceifolia form consanguinea (Merr.) Bakh.
D. mindanensis, Merr.
D. neurosepala, Makh.
D. piscicapa, Ridley
D. soporifera, Bakh.
D. toposioides, King & Gamble
D. Wallichii, King & Gamble

Refs. Burkill, p. 825.

Bakhuizen, Revisio Ebenacearum Malayensium, Bull. Jard. Bot. Buitenzorg 1936 - 1941.

2. T. buah kantu.   Croton tiglium, Linn.

A very large genus of trees, shrubs, and herbs of the family Euphorbiaceae. This species is the

most powerful purgative known. It is a shrub or
small tree, which came from the Himalayas and
southern China, southwards through Malaysia to
the Philippines and New Guinea.

Planted by the Ibans in hill-padi farms. The
poison is obtained by pounding the fruit. The Iban
genetic name for the genus Croton is 'sentupak'.

Ref. Burkill, p. 690.

3. T. 'empadi'   Dioscorea piscatorum, Prain &
                  Burkill

4. T. 'keliting' or   Dioscorea hispida, Dennst.
   'penangat'   (Syn. D. triphylla, Linn.)

This is a large genus of herbaceous, or slightly
woody climbers of the family Dioscoreaceae,
found throughout the moist tropics, and best known
for their tubers which are known as yams.

D. piscatorum is a rather large climber, with
six inch simple leaves, found wild on the lower
slopes of hills in Malaya and Borneo. In Sabah it
is called 'tuba sakut'. Flesh of mature tubers
red.

D. hispida is the most important famine-food
of the East, but the tubers are very poisonous and

before they can be eaten the poison has to be washed out. Recognize by the large tri-foliate leaf. Planted by Ibans. Its use as a fish poison is surrounded by pantangs. One of these is that the name 'keliting' must not be used during tuba fishing - the name 'penangat' is then used.

Ref. Gdns. Bull. Vol.111, p.260 for D. piscatorum Burkill, p. 818 - 823.

5. T. 'kulit kayu' or   Calophyllum mucigerum
   'Bekakal'.   Boerl. & Koord.

A rather large genus of trees of the family Guttiferae, best known in Sarawak for the 'bintangor' timber obtained from the trees.

The only species recorded as a fish poison is C. mucigerum which is not known in Sg. Sut or Sg. Bena but is said to occur up S. Pelagus. The poison is obtained from the bark, and is said to be potent.

6. T. 'langkong'   Barringtonia spp.

A genus of trees of the family Myrtaceae.

B. asiatica, Kurz, is common along sandy shores on the Sarawak coast, and Burkill (p.304) states that the fruits are used in many places as a fish poison.

Ukits mix the poison with Ipoh poison for blowpipe darts. They probably obtain the poison from: -

 B. megistophylla, Merr.) These are Bornean
 B. dolichophylla, Merr.) species not included in Burkill.

7. T.'rumput kachang'
(not known in Kapit district.)

8. T.'sating' Linostoma pauciflora, Griff.

A very small genus of shrubs of the family Thymelaeaceae. This species is identified by the small leaf.

Ref. Burkill, p. 1451.

9. 'Gurah' (Malay name) Sapium indicum, Willd.

A rather large genus of trees and shrubs of the family Euphorbiaceae, found through the tropics.

S. indicum is found all along the sea-coasts of India and throughout Malaysia.

Burkill, p. 1961, states that pounded fruits thrown into water kill the fish in it, and Beccari

("Wanderings in the great forests of Borneo", p. 241) states that it is used at Kuching. Being a coastal tree its use is evidently not known to Ibans.

Burkill, p. 977, states that some species of the genus Euphorbia are fish poisons and quotes K. Heyne as recording that Teijsman found E. antiquorum, Linn., to be maintained in cultivation in West Borneo in order that its latex might be used for fish poison. But so far as we know at present, the Ibans do not use any species of Euphorbia.

10. T.'manbong laut'

A white flowered herb growing eight feet tall in young 'temuda'. Not yet collected or identified.

APPENDIX C

FRESH-WATER FISH

The following list gives the names of the commoner fresh-water fish, including those suitable and usually stocked in fish ponds. The list was provided by Mr. Ong Kee Bian, of the Agriculture Department. The Department has published booklets in Iban, Malay and Chinese on the construction and care of fish ponds.

Chinese Carp (Fry imported from Singapore or Hong Kong)

1. Chow Hu   Ctenopharyngodon idellus

2. Lian Hu   Hypophthalmichthys molitrix

3. Song Hu   Aristichthys nobilis

LIST OF LOCAL FRESH-WATER FISHES

	MALAY	IBAN	LATIN
1.	Mata Merah	Mata Merah	Puntius orphoides
2.	Megalan	Megalan	Puntius sp
3.	Empurau	Empurau	
4.	Tengadak	Tengadak	Puntius bramoides
5.	Bantak	Bantak	Osteochilus vittatus
6.	Semah	Semah	Tor sp
7.	Ikan Puteh (Enpait)	Pait/Bagah	Puntius sp
8.	Boeng	Boeng	Cyclocheilichthys sp
9.	Dungan	Adong	Hampala sp
10.	Baong	Baong	Wallago sp
11.	Tapah	Tapah	Wallago sp
12.	Keli	Keli	Clarias sp
13.	Aruan	Kedubok)	
14.	Blau	Blau/Toman)	Ophicephalus
15.	Teong	Runtu)	
16.	Seluang	Enseluai	Rasbora sp
17.	Seluang	Lansi	Rasbora sp
18.	Labang	Labang	Pangasius sp
19.	Lajong	Lajong	Pangasius sp
20.	Tilan	Tilan	Mastacembelus sp
21.	Betok	Puyu	Anabus Testudineus

22.	Sepat Padi Sepat Padi	Trichogaster trichopterus
23.	Betutu Betutu	Oxyeleotric marmorata
24.	Kalui (Pond Kalui Fish)	Osphronemus gouramy

(Species 1-8 are suitable for stocking ponds)

POND FISH

LOCAL NAME	LATIN
1. Sepat Siam	Trichogaster pectoralis
2. Biawan	Helostoma temmincki
3. Kalui	Osphronemus gouramy
4. Tilapia	Tilapia mossambica
5. Lee Koh	Cyprinus carpio
6. Chit Hu	Carassius auratus
7. Lampan Jawa	Puntius javanicu.

(Fry of 1-6 are available from:- Freshwater Fisheries Division, Department of Agriculture)

APPENDIX D

GLOSSARY OF OTHER WORDS
(used in the text and not explained there)

Local Name

Babai: Forest tree (unidentified).

Belian: 'Ironwood', used for heavy construction, roof shingles, etc., sinks in water; (Eusideroxylon zwageri, T. et B.).

Bemban: Round stemmed reed, growing five feet tall in marshy places; small leaves on short branches at tip, scented white flowers; dried skin of stem is made into mats.

Blachan: Fermented fish paste used as seasoning or fried with spices as a side-dish; best made of very small prawns. Bintulu and Belawai are known for it.

Daun pait;
  and
Daun tubu: Wild leaves used for flavouring, (unidentified). 'Tubu' means bamboo shoots, but this leaf has no connexion. 'Pait' means bitter: the leaf is known in the Rejang, not in 2nd Division.

Emplasi: Small, very active fish (cf., English 'minnow'); the word is used to describe a flighty girl.

Engkabang: General name for illipe nuts and the trees that bear them; common on river banks. There are several kinds, all dipterocarps. Shorea sp., the largest, used in commerce being E. jantong, (gysbertsiana, Burck.), and one of the smaller, used in the home for its finer fat, Tegelam (S. seminis).

Enseluai: Small fish (Malay, 'seluang') suitable for ponds (rashora Sp.)

Entenang: Tree (unidentified), providing fibre for lines and cords.

Kara: Tree (ficus sp.) often strangling a host tree.

Keladi: Vegetable of arum family (Arum colocasia) (caladium), with furry leaf to which water does not cling; hence 'daun keladi' is used (Malay) of a person who makes acquintance but never a close, or lasting, friend.

Kesak: (Malay, 'keringga'), the red weaver ant.

Kikat: A tree fibre for fine cordage (unidentified).

Kemusu: Wasp (unidentified).

Langgir: Tree with grey smooth bark, medium size; bearing an inferior fruit, greenish white but otherwise like a mangosteen to look at (Malay 'kandis', garcinia sp.) The dried skins are pounded fine to make an astringent infusion for use as a hair wash and, with a type of turmeric ('entemut'), in place of soap.

Maram: A kind of rotan cane (Zalacca concerta)

Pantak: Wasp or hornet (unidentified).

Pedalai: Tree with broad indented leaf, bearing poor fruit (probably Atocarpus elastica, Reinw.) Like the jackfruit tree, the bark carries a latex.

Pendok: Small forest tree with pale smooth bark (Cyathocalyx).

Pulai: Pronounced 'pali' in Sarawak. Tree with soft, light wood, having latex used as adulterant of 'jelutong' (chicle "rubber"), preserved by Land Dayaks at the sites of rituals, and by others as an occasional home of wild bees, (Alstonia sp: – A. spathulata, Be., A. angustifolia, Miq., and A. angustifolia, Wall.).

Resam: (Dayak = 'demam'). Bracken (Gleichenia linearis, Barm.). Mature stems are stripped for the fibre which is strong if not expected to be pliable: used for turk's head whippings on scabbards and for black bracelets.

Ridan: (Salacca glabrescens, Griff.)

Samak: Tannin preservative and stain extracted from the bark of several species of trees, both hill and swamp. Swamp species (Rhizophora, Bruguiera, 'bakau') are used commercially.

Tengang: Tree yielding fibre for cords (unidentified).

Ulu: The head waters of a river, the hilly area far up-river.

APPENDIX E

FISHING

'SAGANG': a method of catching small fish used by Malays (in the Saribas) in the fast-running muddy tidal waters. The boat is anchored as the tide rises and a fine conical net is rigged each side of the boat so that it can be lifted easily. The nets are about eighteen inches or two feet across the rim at the mouth and three or four feet deep.

LOG-TRAPS: a very large trap is called 'abau', which may be as much as thirty feet long. It is used at the lower end of a stretch of river being fished with poison.

Another method of using these traps is that used for catching 'keli' or catfish (clarias batrachus s. magur). When the moon has waned two nights ('keleman keli'), catfish can be caught in a log-trap if the trap is baited with red weaver-ants and dropped into the water. It must not be left in too long or the fish will take the bait and get out again. The method is called 'nengklap' in the Skrang.

THORN-TRAP: This is usually baited with leaves, such as tapioca leaves.

TAKE-LINES ('ginti ujak') can be used for catfish in swampy streams such as the Tisak (in the Lower Skrang) Skrang people call the method 'nyagang'.

PUSH-NETS: ('ambei'). A similar net, but smaller, can be used by a man wading where the bank is not steep nor the water too deep. The method is used also along the seashore for prawns and such: Melanaus call it 'pakak'.

All items except the first, 'sagang', collected with the following at Rumah Penghulu Abok, Sebauh, Bintulu, where the people are from the Skrang.

TRAPS FOR SMALL ANIMALS

'PETOK' for squirrels and rats. This consists of a noose inside a bamboo with the trip cord through holes to cross the bamboo and the noose. The trip cord must be bitten to get at the bait: release of the trigger causes the noose to tighten and hold the animal inside the bamboo.

'PANJOK TALING' (weighted noose) is the opposite to 'petok' and has a noose set round a log. The weight of an animal running along the log springs the trap and the noose holds him fast to the log.

'TERINGKAP' is similar but does not use a noose. Instead, springing the trap causes a heavy log to fall upon the trip log, and pin down or crush the animal.

CPSIA information can be obtained
at www.ICGtesting.com
Printed in the USA
BVOW08s1240111216
470466BV00001B/49/P

9 781444 655322